TOUR GUIDE

FLORIDA

Produced by AA Publishing

CONTENTS

Written by Paul Murphy
Copy editor: Janet Tabinski
Edited, designed, produced and distributed by AA Publishing, Fanum House, Basingstoke, Hampshire RG21 2EA.
© The Automobile Association 1992.
Maps © The Automobile Association 1992.

A CIP catalogue record for this book is available from the British Library.
ISBN 0 7495 0435 8
Typesetting: Wyvern Typesetting, Bristol
Colour separation: Mullis Morgan Ltd, London
Printed and bound in Italy by Printers S.R.L., Trento

The contents of this publication are believed correct at the time of printing. Nevertheless, the publishers cannot accept responsibility for errors or omissions, or for changes in details given.

Every effort has been made to ensure accuracy in this guide. However, things do change and we would welcome any information to help keep the book up to date.

Published by AA Publishing
Cover picture: *Riviera Beach*
Title page: *Key West Beach*
Above: *Beware, 'gators crossing!*
Right: *Disney's Sorcery in the Sky (Copyrighted)*

INTRODUCTION

This book is not only a practical touring guide for the independent traveler, but is also invaluable for those who would like to know more about Florida. ~

It is divided into 7 regions, each with its own city tours and motor tours. These start and finish in those cities which we consider to be the best centers for exploration.

The 9 major city tours are designed to show you them at their best, and there are special features on the Everglades, Walt Disney World and Spaceport USA.

Each motor tour has details of the most interesting places to visit en route. Side panels cater for special interests and requirements and cover a range of categories—for those whose interest is in history, wildlife or walking, and those who have children. There are also panels which highlight scenic stretches of road along the route and which give details of special events, crafts and customs. These are cross-referred back to the main text. The simple route directions are accompanied by an easy-to-use map of the tour and there are addresses of local tourist information centers in some of the towns en route as well as in the start town. Simple charts show how far it is from one town to the next in miles and kilometers. These can help you to decide where to take a break and stop overnight, for example. (All distances quoted are approximate.)

Before setting off it is advisable to check with the information center at the start of the tour for recommendations on where to break your journey and for additional information on what to see and do, and when best to visit.

ENTRY REGULATIONS

Visas are required by all visitors to the US, except for Canadian citizens, or nationals of Britain, France, Germany, Italy, the Netherlands, Sweden, Switzerland or Japan visiting the US for business or tourist purposes, for a stay not exceeding 90 days, and provided that a return, or onward, ticket is held. In these instances a passport only is required. It is best to check the requirements for specific holiday plans before departure. The type and validity of US visas vary considerably, so seek advice from the nearest US Embassy or Consulate. American immigration officials are strict in these matters and passengers whose travel documents are not in order will not be accepted in the US under any circumstances.

BANKS

As a general rule, banks are open from 9am to 3pm Monday to Friday and are closed on weekends and public holidays, although in some tourist areas hours may be longer. Currency may be changed at airports and some hotels, but it is best to take US dollar travelers' checks. Hotels, restaurants, gas (petrol) stations and shops in Florida will accept them as cash and give change where necessary.

CREDIT CARDS

You can use credit cards almost anywhere. All the major credit cards are widely used and accepted throughout Florida.

CURRENCY

The American monetary unit is the dollar ($) which is divided into 100 cents (¢). Coins are issued in cent denominations of 1 (penny), 5 (nickel), 10 (dime), 25 (quarter) and 50 (half-dollar). Notes (bills) are issued in denominations of one, two, five, 10, 20, 50 and 100 dollars. All bills, whatever their value, are exactly the same size and color. The value of the bill is clearly shown in all corners and each has its own US statesman pictured in the center.

HEALTH

It cannot be emphasized enough that arranging medical insurance before traveling is essential. Medical facilities are generally of an extremely high standard, but costs in the US are exorbitant so it is well worth taking out insurance cover beforehand. An insurance cover for an unlimited amount of medical costs is recommended. Treatment (unless an emergency) will be refused without evidence of insurance or a deposit. If you need a doctor during your stay, ask at your hotel or look in the Yellow Pages under 'Physician'. No inoculations are required for a visit

The architectural heavyweights of glass and chromium jostle for supremacy on the Miami city skyline

The turrets and spires of a living dream – Cinderella's Castle

to Florida, but it is a rabies risk area. Tap water is generally safe to drink.

EMERGENCY TELEPHONE NUMBERS

There is no nationwide emergency system in the US. There are emergency numbers you can call, and these are sometimes indicated on pay phones, but they vary from place to place. In Florida, in any emergency, it is best to call the police, who will put you in contact with the appropriate service if they cannot help—dial 911 (free call) in the Miami, Orlando and Tampa areas. Otherwise the best thing to do is call the operator by dialing '0' and ask to be connected.

CUSTOMS REGULATIONS

Non-US residents may bring in up to one liter of alcoholic beverages (if they are 21 or over), 200 cigarettes (or 50 cigars or 3lb of tobacco) plus up to $100 worth of gifts (including 100 cigars) in addition to the tobacco allowance. There is no limit to the amount of currency (US or foreign) brought into America, but arriving and departing passengers must report to US customs all money in excess of $10,000. Not allowed: fresh meat, fruit, drugs (other than prescribed), and plants.

POST OFFICES

Post office hours vary both in central city branches and in small towns, so it is best to check. Stamps, however, may be purchased in hotels, motels, drugstores and transport terminals, usually by inserting correct change into a machine, though these charge 25 percent more.

TELEPHONES

Exact change in 5, 10 or 25 cent coins is needed to place a call (minimum of 25 cents). Florida has a direct-dial system. The state is divided into four telephone regions, with the area codes of 305, 407, 813 and 904. For direct dialing international calls dial 011, plus country code, plus city code, plus telephone number. Country codes for international calls:

Australia 61
Canada 1
New Zealand 64
UK 44

TIME

Most of Florida is on Eastern Standard Time; for most of the year 5 hours behind Britain, 6 hours behind the rest of Western Europe and 15 hours behind Australia (Sydney). Part of the northwest, including Pensacola and Fort Walton Beach, is on Central Time, an hour behind the rest of Florida.

MOTORING

Documents

You need a valid driving license to rent a car in Florida, though an International Driver's Permit is required for visitors from certain countries. Usually you must be 21 or over.

Breakdowns

The American Automobile Association (AAA) is a member of a worldwide association of motoring organizations (AIT) and as such makes certain services available to visitors of member organizations. The Triple A operates a nationwide road service number to assist you in the US: call 1-800-222-7764 and you will be given information for obtaining emergency assistance. Should you break down on a highway lift up the hood (bonnet) of your car and remain in the vehicle until the Highway Patrol arrives. Do not open your doors or windows to anyone else.

Accidents

If you are involved in a traffic accident it must be reported to the local police station, County Sheriff's Office, or Florida Highway Patrol at once. Exchange names, addresses and insurance details. If someone is injured or you are held responsible, insist on contacting your embassy or consulate.

Route directions

Throughout the book the following abbreviations are used for US roads:

I–Interstate Highway
US–US Highway
SR–State Route
CR–County Route

Speed limits

The speed limit on Florida highways is 55–65mph (88–105km/h).

The Orlando banking conglomerates concentrate their might around Lake Eola Park, with the Orlando Centennial Fountain piercing the intervening space

---

PUBLIC HOLIDAYS

1 January–New Year's Day
15 January–Martin Luther King Day
3rd Monday in February–Washington's Birthday
last Monday in May–Memorial Day
4 July–Independence Day
1st Monday in September–Labor Day
2nd Monday in October–Columbus Day
11 November–Veterans Day
4th Thursday in November–Thanksgiving Day
25 December–Christmas Day

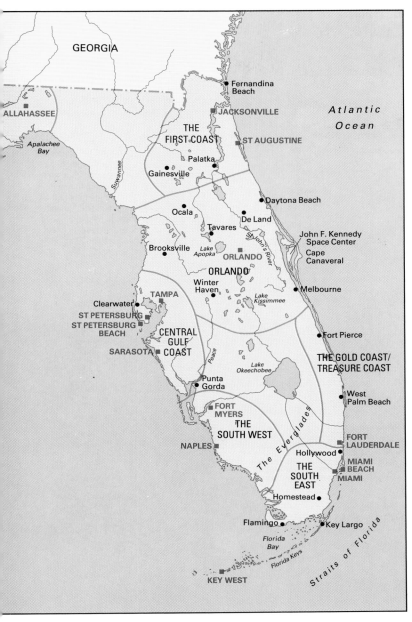

GEORGIA

Fernandina
Beach

JACKSONVILLE

*Atlantic
Ocean*

ALLAHASSEE

THE
FIRST COAST

ST AUGUSTINE

*Apalachee
Bay*

Suwannee

Palatka

Gainesville

Daytona Beach

Ocala

De Land

Tavares

St John's River

John F. Kennedy
Space Center

Brooksville   *Lake
Apopka*   ORLANDO

Cape
Canaveral

ORLANDO

Winter
Haven

*Lake
Kissimmee*

Melbourne

TAMPA

Clearwater

ST PETERSBURG
ST PETERSBURG
BEACH

SARASOTA

CENTRAL
GULF
COAST

Peace

*Lake
Okeechobee*

Fort Pierce

THE GOLD COAST/
TREASURE COAST

Punta
Gorda

West
Palm Beach

FORT
MYERS

THE
SOUTH WEST

NAPLES

The Everglades

Hollywood

FORT
LAUDERDALE

MIAMI
BEACH

THE
SOUTH
EAST

MIAMI

Homestead

Flamingo

Key Largo

*Florida
Bay*

Florida Keys

Straits of Florida

KEY WEST

In cities and congested areas though it is generally 20–40mph (32–64km/h) and 15mph (24km/h) in school zones. Road signs indicate specific limits and those are strictly enforced.

Driving conditions
Florida, like the rest of the US, has an extensive system of freeways (motorways) and highways (other roads). Superhighways are toll roads charging a few cents a mile and gas (petrol) remains more reasonable than in many other destinations. Driving is on the right.

Car hire and fly-drive
Each hire firm offers its own packages and discounts, but in any case car hire is cheaper in this state than in any other. When it comes to paying, it should be noted that some car rental companies will *not* accept cash — you will need one of the major credit cards. Also there may be an under-25 surcharge.

Some flight operators feature fly-drive programmes here, often including free use of a car for a spe-cific period. The vast majority of hire cars are automatics.

Collision Damage Waiver (CDW) is essential. Without this you could be liable for any damage to your vehicle, however caused, or even the full cost should the car be stolen. This can be arranged independently.

Driving tips
Two peculiarities to American driving are that it is permitted for a motorist to filter right at a red traffic light after stopping (a flashing red light means stop, then proceed with caution in any direction), and that traffic in both directions must stop while a school bus is loading or unloading.

It is compulsory for children under five to be seated in a special child seat or restraint — your car-rental firm should be able to supply one for a small additional charge. Front seat-belts are compulsory for all passengers.

Always carry your driving license on your person in case you are stopped.

TOURIST OFFICES

For information in the US on the whole of the state of Florida contact:
Office of Visitor Inquiry, Florida Division of Tourism, 126 West Van Buren Street, Tallahasee, FL 32399-2000. *Tel*: (904) 487-1462.
The Florida Division of Tourism operates visitor centers in major towns and resorts and at various roadside locations. For more specific information, ask at the local Chamber of Commerce.

ELECTRICITY

The standard electricity supply in the US is 110–120 volts (60 cycles). You may have to bring an adaptor to convert. Sockets take plugs with two flat pins.

CONSULATES

The only British consulate in Florida is in Miami, at Suite 2110, Bricknell Bay Office Tower, 1001 S Bayshore Drive, *tel*: (305) 374-1522.

THE SOUTH EAST

For adult visitors at least, the southeast corner of Florida, stretching from Miami Beach to Key West, is the most exciting part of the whole state. The place-names alone conjure up expectant magic, and even if the myth sometimes doesn't match the reality (neither the Everglades nor the streets of Miami are as wild as you might have thought), few vacationers leave disappointed. The contrasts here are as vivid as the subtropical colors. Immigrants flock here from both hemispheres – senior citizens fleeing south from the cold northern states, refugees fleeing north from political turmoil in Cuba, Haiti and Nicaragua. Modern building developments, fueled by the tourist dollar, push ahead apace and, just a few miles separate sophisticated metropolitan suburbs from backwoods airboat shanties, glass-and-concrete canyons from deserted tropical islands, the Wall Street of the South from conch shell-blowing competitions. Southeast Florida works hard but also relaxes with some panache and all the vitality that its rich multiethnic mix has brought with it.

The man who put Miami and the Florida Keys on the map was Henry Morrison Flagler, railroad magnate and cofounder of the Standard Oil Company. In the 1890s he drove his railroad to the remote outposts of the mosquito-bitten south, inspired, so legend has it, by frost-free orange blossom sent to him from Miami. Flagler, envisaging trade with neighboring Cuba and the Caribbean, pushed on ever southwards, and the 'railroad that went to sea' finally made it to Key West in 1912.

The devastating hurricane of 1935 sent the railroad and over 400 unfortunate souls with it to a watery grave, but by then the die was cast. 'Flagler's Folly' was never reconstructed, but it provided a valuable base for the Overseas Highway that now links the Keys.

Other tycoons followed Flagler, and rapid uncontrolled land development led to cycles of boom and bust that still occur today. Nevertheless, by the 1920s the sunniest part of the Sunshine State had become America's biggest vacation playground. Since then it has suffered the vagaries of economic depression, shifting fashions and all manner of other problems, including crime epidemics. In true Florida style, however, the wheel has come full circle, and once again the southeast is undoubtedly the place to be.

City Tour 1
The vibrant business and cultural hub of the region, the city has now largely shaken off the seamier side of its *Miami Vice* image while retaining its style and glamor. The new monorail Metromover train makes skyscraper-spotting easy and enjoyable, while the Bayside complex is a must for eating, drinking and shopping.

City Tour 2
Art Deco hotels, washed in pastel shades, facing a golden beach, are the quintessential image of Miami Beach. At one time considered quite tasteless and so neglected as to become downright seedy during the 1970s, the Beach and its buildings have been extensively transformed over the last decade into the city's hottest spot.

Tour 1
The tour of the southern suburbs emphasizes how multicultural and cosmopolitan Miami has become:

Spanish architecture at Coral Gables, European sidewalk cafés and Bahamian lifestyles at Coconut Grove, Cuba transplanted at Calle Ocho. There is also a wealth of first-class tourist attractions for all tastes, including historic houses, wildlife parks, botanical gardens, beaches and shopping.

Tour 2
The northern suburbs will show you something of everyday Miami, yet here too there are colorful ethnic neighborhoods, exclusive beach communities to explore and tourist attractions unique to the state.

Tour 3
You can 'do' the Everglades in a day from Miami along the Tamiami Trail, but if you want to see more than a few alligators and an air-

The skyscrapers of the Miami skyline at nightfall are metamorphosed into giant Christmas trees of light

boat, take the longer tour to Flamingo, stop off at the board-walks en route and stay overnight. If you have any affinity for nature, you will find it well worthwhile.

Tour 4
The Keys tour is a must for water enthusiasts, but even at under-water havens such as the excellent John Pennekamp State Park, you don't need gills to enjoy the only living coral reef in the US. At the end of the line is Key West.

City Tour 3
Just 90 miles (145km) north of Cuba, this tiny jewel is, not surprisingly, more Caribbean than North American. Its culture and atmosphere are very laid back and very bohemian. Nevertheless, there is plenty to see and do here, both on and off the water, and just taking in the street architecture is a delight. The tour comes to a fitting climax at Mallory Square, watching Key West's street performers pay homage to the golden sunset.

DOWNTOWN MIAMI

Bayside Marketplace • Southeast Financial Center
CenTrust Tower • Flagler Street
Dade County Courthouse
Metro-Dade Cultural Center • Freedom Tower
Miami Dade Community College
Bayside Marketplace

Although downtown Miami lies a mere bridge away from South Beach, its high-rise city canyons of reflective glass and stern gray stone seem a world removed from the tropical pastel shades by the oceanfront. On Brickell Avenue alone lies the greatest concentration of banking business outside of New York, and if skyscraper altitude is any indicator of serious intent —as it seems to be in major US cities—then Miami is a heavyweight contender.

Two recent developments have made downtown both very accessible and very appealing to all Miami visitors. The first is the *Metromover*, a fully automated shuttle train that runs on an elevated 1.9-mile (3km) loop through the heart of the business district. Fares are cheap and stops are frequent, so you can hop on and off at will. The second is the outstanding tourist-oriented *Bayside Marketplace*, a shopping and entertainment complex. Visit downtown Miami by day when it bustles with lawyers and bankers, but don't miss viewing it by night when its mighty rainbow-lit towers form Florida's greatest cityscape.

SPECIAL TO . . .

For one day in February each year, the executive BMWs and Mercedes of the downtown business district clear the streets for seriously fast racing cars to take part in the **Miami Grand Prix**. The circuit, which goes out to Key Biscayne, has special spectator seating erected along Biscayne Boulevard.

ⓘ Greater Miami Convention and Visitors Bureau, Brickell Avenue

Start the tour at Bayside Marketplace.

Bayside Marketplace

1 This ebullient waterfront complex of shops, restaurants and general entertainment, recently completed at a cost of almost $100 million, has already become a favorite focal point. Whether you enjoy shopping or not, this is an ideal introduction to the colorful and vibrant multiethnic Miami scene. There is an excellent choice of eating places to suit all tastes and pockets, the shops offer a wide selection of high-quality arts, crafts and fashion clothing at reasonable prices, and the atmosphere is never less than lively thanks to the ever present street entertainers. Fully rigged tallships are always at berth here, and for a few pieces of silver you can even board a full-size replica of **HMS** *Bounty*. There is a whole fleet of modern yachts to see at the adjacent **Miamarina,** with over 200

Let the sun shine in: a glass-roofed restaurant at Bayside Marketplace

berths, and you can cruise the bay and coast in any number of vessels, including an oversize Venetian gondola. If you are here in April, don't miss **Miami Magic**, a light-and-laser show held in front of the Marketplace in Bayfront Park.

Cross the street and walk a few hundred yards left down Biscayne Boulevard.

Southeast Financial Center

2 At 55 stories (and a cost of $200 million) this is the tallest building in Florida. Walk below through its 1-acre (0.4-hectare) plaza and gaze up at the mini plantation of royal palms, which tower up toward a crisscrossed 'space canopy' of glass and steel.

Walk back toward Bayside and board the Metromover at Bayfront Park station. Alight at Knight Center station.

CenTrust Tower

3 Another monument to Miami's financial status, the CenTrust Tower is smaller than the Southeast Financial Center at 47 stories, but has a higher cultural rating as it boasts the **J L Knight Concert Hall.** Look for the CenTrust at night when it is brilliantly illuminated. Often red, white and blue, it changes seasonally (red and green at Christmas, purple and pink at Easter)—and when the tower turns orange, you know that the Miami Dolphins football team is at home.

At Knight Center station transfer to the inner loop and get off at Miami Avenue station. Walk north on North Miami Avenue to Flagler Street.

Flagler Street

4 Before the advent of suburban malls, Flagler Street was Miami's main shopping street. Although there is a **Burdine's** department store here, the emphasis is now on business to business, and the area is one of the country's leading import-export centers. Come here if you are interested in audio, video or photographic equipment.

Return to the Metromover and travel clockwise, getting off at Government Center station. Walk south on NW 1st Avenue.

Dade County Courthouse

5 This Miami landmark, with its distinctive ziggurat roof, was the tallest building south of Washington DC when completed in 1928. It remained the tallest building in Miami until the 1970s. As dusk falls and its colony of roosting turkey vultures soars around its pyramidal peak, it takes on a rather sinister appearance. The public can sit in on court sessions.

Cross the street.

Metro-Dade Cultural Center

6 An architectural mix of Modernism and Spanish Revivalism, this block holds the **Center for the Fine Arts** and the **Historical Museum of Southern Florida.** The former features two stories of the very best in touring exhibitions, changing every two months, plus a sculpture court. The latter is probably more accessible for all the family and takes an entertaining look at the settlement of Florida by means of large-scale recreations (walk through a Spanish fort, restored exhibits (board a Miami trolley car), plus tableaux, audiovisuals and hands-on displays. The outdoor plaza here is a good place for a cup of coffee, with a 360-degree view of some of Miami's tallest structures.

Return to the Metromover. Travel clockwise and get off at Edcom station. Walk east along NE 5th Street. Turn left onto NE 2nd Avenue, then right onto NE 6th Street.

Freedom Tower

7 This Spanish-Mediterranean-style tower was built in 1925 for the *Miami Daily News* as a replica of the Giralda Tower in Seville. It acquired its present name in 1962, when it was used as an emergency refugee-processing center during the period of flight from Castro's Cuba. (Not open to the public.)

Return to the Metromover. Travel clockwise and get off at College Bayside station.

Miami Dade Community College

8 The Mitchell Wolfson Jr Gallery here features an interesting collection of decorative and propaganda art from 1875 to 1945 (due to move to the Art Deco district in 1992 and reopen under the name Museum of

The Metromover arcs past the strongly linear CenTrust Tower

Propaganda Arts). The **Frances Wolfson Art Gallery** is a contemporary showcase for Miami's ethnic communities. It is indicative of Miami's multiethnicity that an annual Haitian festival is held here in May. (College open weekdays only.)

Either take the Metromover and travel clockwise to return to Bayfront Park station, or walk the short distance to and along Biscayne Boulevard.

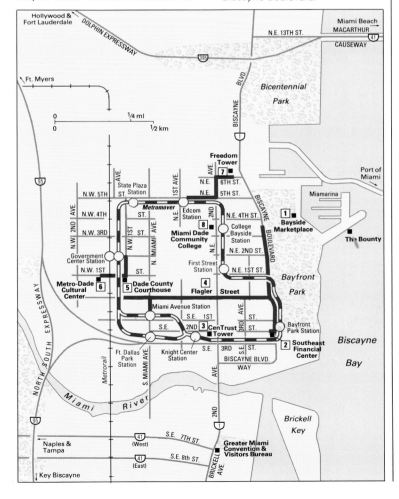

MIAMI BEACH

South Pointe Park • Joe's Stone Crab Restaurant
Art Deco District
Stephen Muss Convention Center
Bass Museum of Art • Fontainebleau Hilton Resort
South Pointe Park

A fine example of Miami Beach's many colorful Art Deco buildings

The Miami Beach area first became fashionable in the 1920s. The combination of a luxurious subtropical retreat and frontier opportunities lured tycoons, who in turn sought to attract tourists by creating a fantasy land where they could forget their cold northern climes and the Great Depression. Art Deco, a style brought over from an international art exhibition in Paris in 1925, was the perfect artistic vehicle for the purpose. This style is typified by pastel shades, neon strips, and futuristic streamlined shapes, as well as motifs from ancient civilizations and shapes from the natural world.

Since the creation of the district, which boasts about 800 buildings over 1 square mile (2.5 sq km), much has happened to the fortunes of Miami Beach, and it was not until 1979 that the city decided to protect this valuable asset by having it nationally listed as a historic district. The result is a return to high fashion, complete with the hottest night clubs, the classiest hotels and some of the best restaurants in town.

SPECIAL TO ...

The best time to visit the Art Deco district is in mid-January during the annual **Art Deco Weekend**, a three-day festival during which the whole area goes into a pastel-tinged 1930s time warp. Vendors sell period clothing and antiques at a street fair, vintage automobiles cruise the streets, and the finale is a **'Moon over Miami' ball**.

BACK TO NATURE

Escape the hustle and bustle of the Beach at the **Miami Beach Garden and Conservatory**, which adjoins the Convention Center. Here, exotic native earth and air plants flourish under a dome 32 feet (10m) high.

ℹ Welcome Center, 661 Washington Avenue (Art Deco district)

From downtown Miami cross the MacArthur Causeway (US 41). Turn right onto Alton Road.

South Pointe Park

1 This is the start of **South Miami Beach ('SoBe')**—3 miles (5km) of fine golden sands popular with stunt-kite flyers, swimmers, surfers and windsurfers.

The southernmost tip is a favorite spot for fishing and also for watching the big boats entering and leaving the **Port of Miami**, the world's largest cruise ship port. **Friday Night Live** (from rock to classical music), held weekly in the small amphitheater here, is just one of the many outdoor concerts held at the beach.

As you leave the park, turn right on Biscayne Street.

Joe's Stone Crab Restaurant

2 The most famous restaurant in Miami, and possibly the state, Joe's is a fourth-generation family business, opened in 1913. The meal that has passed into Florida folklore here is stone crabs with mustard sauce, garlic spinach and hash browns. Always busy and often hectic. Reservations are not accepted, so arrive early to avoid a lengthy wait. The restaurant is closed from mid-May to mid-October, when stone crabs are out of season.

Take Ocean Drive to 6th Street.

Art Deco District

3 The famous square mile starts here, running north–south as far as 23rd Street. **Ocean Drive** contains many of the best examples of Art Deco styling and, with the revival of the area, has established itself as one of Miami's trendiest strips. Everyone has his own favorite buildings, but look out for the classic lines of the **Cardozo**, the **Park Central** and the **Cleveland** hotels, and step into a lobby or two to admire the period fixtures and furnishings. To see most of the rest of the area, turn left onto Collins Avenue at 13th and head south back to 5th Street, then turn right onto Washington Avenue and head north again. The Spanish-themed, gas-lit **Española Way** (a favorite *Miami Vice* backdrop) and the Lincoln Road Arts District, both just off Washington, are also worth exploring.

Continue north on Washington Avenue.

Stephen Muss Convention Center

4 This huge Art Deco-faced building is home to several major annual events including two boat shows (February and July), two auto shows (April and November) and the Antique Show (January). Next door to the center, on Convention Center Drive, is **Miami Beach City Hall**, built in 1927 and referred to as the doyen of Art Deco architecture. Adjacent on Washington Avenue is the **Jackie Gleason Theater of the Performing Arts**, which produces the best of Broadway and classical concerts.

Turn right onto Park Avenue.

Bass Museum of Art

5 This cultural centerpiece of Miami Beach is housed in a handsome gray coral-rock, Art Deco-style building. Its splendid collection ranges from modern American masters, such as Roy Lichtenstein, back six centuries through ecclesiastic art, huge Flemish tapestries and a large body of works by European masters such as Rubens, Rembrandt and Toulouse-Lautrec. Changing exhibitions augment the permanent collection.

Turn right onto 22nd Street and left onto Collins Avenue.

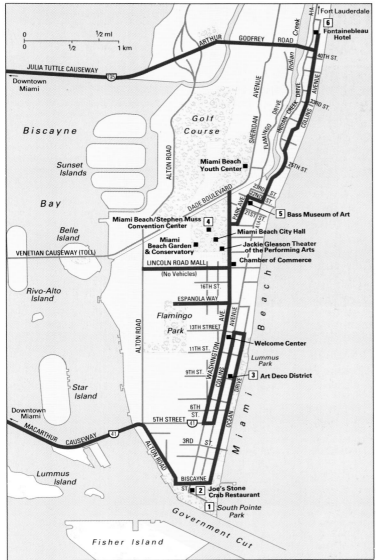

In the winter of 1895 Julia Tuttle, the pioneering woman after whom the causeway is named, convinced Henry Flagler to build his railroad down to the remote outpost of Miami by sending him freshly picked Miami orange blossom. While every other producing town in the state of Florida had just lost its crop to an exceptional freeze, Miami's mild climate had kept its produce virtually frost-free.

FOR CHILDREN

Apart from the pleasures of the beach itself, the **Miami Beach Youth Center** (south end of Sheridan Avenue, one block east of Flamingo Drive) offers an ice-skating park, six bowling alleys, a swimming pool, and three tennis courts, plus supervised activities for children of all ages.

RECOMMENDED WALKS

Join a guide from the **Miami Design Preservation League** at the Welcome Center, 661 Washington Avenue, at 10.30 on Saturday mornings for a 90-minute walking tour of the Art Deco square mile. You will learn who built what, when, why, how much the buildings originally cost (and what they are worth today) and a whole host of trivia, including the hotels where you could have glimpsed many famous names. For a more relaxed stroll in an area devoid of buildings, head for the boardwalk, which stretches for 2 miles (3km) between 21st and 46th streets.

Fontainebleau Hilton Resort

6 Just before arriving at this Miami Beach landmark, you will see looming directly ahead a huge archway, beyond which is a great white sweeping building (the back of the Fontainebleau) set on a tropical lagoon. Don't be tempted to take a short cut, as the archway is a massive *trompe l'oeil*. This giant resort (known locally as 'the Big Blue') boasts over 1,200 rooms, a health spa, seven restaurants, five lounges and any number of sporting facilities. As with all American hotels, the general public is always welcome, so at the very least explore the lounges and lobbies which you will find either artful or kitschy depending on your taste. For an evening of lavish Las Vegas-style entertainment, try the **Club Tropigala**, graced by stars such as Frank Sinatra.

Head back down Collins Avenue and turn right onto Arthur Godfrey Road, which leads via the Julia Tuttle Causeway back to the mainland.

Life on the ocean waves: a cruise ship at the Port of Miami

1 day – 66 miles (107km)

GREATER MIAMI SOUTH

**Bayside Marketplace ● Brickell Avenue
Key Biscayne ● Vizcaya ● Coconut Grove
Bakery Center ● Metrozoo ● Coral Gables
Little Havana ● Bayside Marketplace**

This tour of south suburban Miami contains within a few square miles the number-one zoo and the most splendid stately home in Florida, plus several other natural, marine and wildlife attractions that rank among the very best in the state. This is also a tour of contrasts—from the shimmering downtown skyline to the serene beaches of Key Biscayne, and from the elegant suburbia of refined Coral Gables to robust and earthy Little Havana. Coconut Grove, on the other hand, is the quintessential Miami suburb, a cosmopolitan melting pot of chic European and Bahamian influences. If you are using downtown or Miami Beach as a base for this tour, aim to see two or three attractions per trip. If time is limited the favorites are Vizcaya, Seaquarium, Metrozoo and Coconut Grove. If you don't want to drive, then the *Old Town Trolley Tour* is recommended. The full tour takes 90 minutes and stops at downtown, Seaquarium, Vizcaya, Coconut Grove and Coral Gables before heading back to Bayside Marketplace via Little Havana.

Brilliantly feathered residents of Parrot Jungle, one of Miami's oldest and most popular attractions. The birds fly free in a subtropical setting

ⓘ Greater Miami Convention and Visitors Bureau, Brickell Avenue

Starting at Bayside Marketplace take Brickell Avenue south.

Brickell Avenue

1 As you cross the Miami River, take a look below at the flotilla of business and pleasure craft that sails this busy waterway. Then look skywards to admire the mighty banking structures along Brickell. The soaring 33-story **Barnett Tower** is a domestic flagship, while the striking **Banco de Venezuela**, in stunning jet black, is a reminder of Miami's importance as a Latin American banking center. Serious business soon gives way to colorful residential condominiums; the two real eye-openers are the **Villa Regina**, where every balcony is painted a different pastel shade of the rainbow, and the fabulous 20-story **Atlantis**. The latter is unmistakable with its brilliant mirror surface, its completely rounded ends, and a massive red triangle on the roof; its 'trademark' (familiar to millions of *Miami Vice* fans as a backdrop on the opening credits) is the 'hole-in-the-wall' between its 12th and 16th stories. Inside the hole stands a palm tree and a red circular staircase that leads nowhere.

Turn left onto the Rickenbacker Causeway for 8 miles (13km) to Key Biscayne.

Key Biscayne

2 The peaceful pine groves and semi-tropical beaches on this beautiful island, so close to downtown, make a perfect retreat from the more fashionable sands, and bodies, of Miami Beach. Choose from either the rugged 2-mile (3km) sandy beach of **Virginia Key**, the 800 acres (325 hec-

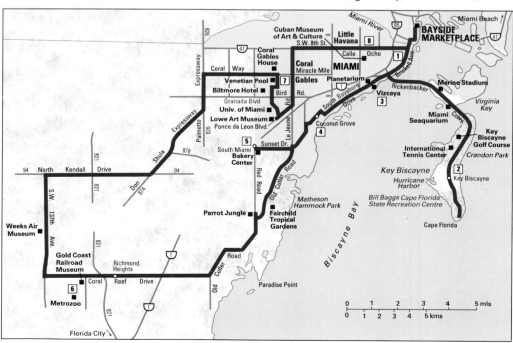

Palatial Vizcaya, built as a winter home for bachelor millionaire James Deering. Its 10 acres (4 hectares) of formal gardens face Biscayne Bay

tares) of wooded parkland and 3 miles (5km) of beach at **Crandon Park** or the mile-long (1.5km) beach at **Bill Baggs Cape Florida State Recreation Area**. Key Biscayne is also a great spot for water thrills. The world's fastest boats compete around the island for the **Miss Budweiser Unlimited Hydroplane Regatta** during two weekends every June. For everyday *Miami Vice*-style speedboat-spotting, try Sundays on the bay at Crandon Boulevard, particularly around brunchtime. If you would like to be a wave-runner, you can rent your own jet skis from Tony's, near the **Marine Stadium. Seaquarium** is the largest and best of south Florida's marine parks, and features Lolita, the 10,000-pound (4,535kg) killer whale. A huge tropical aquarium, sea lion and dolphin shows, plus shark feeding complete at least half a day's educational entertainment for the whole family. A little further on, the **Key Biscayne Golf Course** is one of the country's finest public courses. Close by is the **International Tennis Center**, where many international tournaments are staged, including the prestigious ladies' Lipton's Championship (courts open to the public). Drive to the tip of the key to Bill Baggs Recreation Area, where you can see historical Cape Florida Lighthouse and enjoy a picnic or a barbecue (grills provided) on Key Biscayne's prettiest beach.

Return across the Rickenbacker Causeway and turn left onto South Miami Avenue/South Bayshore Drive for Vizcaya, 8 miles (13km).

Vizcaya

3 Built in 1916 as a winter home for millionaire industrialist James Deering, this magnificent Italianate villa is one of the finest private houses in the US. Its name is Basque, meaning 'elevated ground'. A 50-minute guided tour of the downstairs area will show you opulent European furnishings and decorative arts dating back to the 16th century. You are then free to explore the rest of the villa's 34 public rooms at will. A bed that once belonged to Admiral Nelson's mistress, Lady Hamilton, a complete ceiling from a Venetian ducal palace, and tapestries that were once owned by the English poet Robert Browning are just a few of the eclectic treasures gathered from all over Europe. The splendid gardens, which open out onto the bay, comprise both formal areas and a natural subtropical jungle. President Reagan and Pope John Paul II met in the house and gardens in 1987. One of Miami's most romantic nights is an evening of **Sound and Light** at Vizcaya, when its sculptures, fountains and stained glass are magically transformed as period music rolls back the centuries (reservations necessary). The clock is also turned back some 400 years for two annual festivals, the **Shakespeare Festival** and the **Italian Renaissance Fair**. The latter features a 16th-century marketplace of arts and crafts, music and theater, food and drink.

Continue along South Bayshore Drive for 2 miles (3km).

Coconut Grove

4 Dinner Key Marina heralds the start of 'the Grove' and was the former home of Pan Am's romantic flying boats. Boats and romance still set the tone with fine restaurants and any number of companies renting out

RECOMMENDED WALKS

Within the area bounded by Red Road, the Tamiami Trail (SW 8th Street), Douglas Road and Sunset Drive are a number of 'villages' boasting distinctive national architectural styles, including French (provincial and city), Dutch South African and Chinese. Stop on the **Miracle Mile** to window shop and also to admire **Coral Gables City Hall**, an elegant Spanish Renaissance-style building dating from 1927. There is a charming Congregational church from the same period on Columbus Boulevard, and close by in the northwest corner of the Gables is a series of reflection pools. This covers quite a large area, so if you don't feel up to the walk you can go by bicycle like the natives—the nearest rental is at Coconut Grove.

The views from the Rickenbacker Causeway as you drive back to the mainland are spectacular. The Miami skyline is framed to the right by jet skiers and to the left by windsurfers and anglers. Make the journey by night for an unforgettable view of the city and look out for the 'Miami Line', a 3,600-foot (1,100m) strip of colored lighting strung along the Metrorail bridge next to the CenTrust Tower. Once you get back to the mainland, head north on the elevated section of **I-95** for even better views.

When the palatial splendor of Vizcaya starts to overwhelm the children, just cross the road to the **Museum of Science and Space Transit Planetarium.** This educational discovery center is great fun for both children and parents and features over 150 hands-on exhibits plus a small wildlife section. The planetarium stages astronomy and laser shows, and stargazers can visit its observatory free of charge on weekend evenings.

On Key Biscayne, visit **Bill Baggs Park** and **Bill Baggs Cape Florida State Recreation Area** at the southern tip of the island. Look for brown pelicans, laughing gulls, terns, egrets and waders. During migration times—March to May and September to November—look out for migrant birds.

sailboats at what is now Greater Miami's largest marina. The lovely, leafy suburb of Coconut Grove is the oldest part of Miami, and there are many reminders of its 19th-century origins. Start your tour on Main Highway at the **Barnacle**, built in 1886 and named after the shape of its steep, hipped roof. This was the home of Commodore Ralph Munroe, founder of the Grove, and is open to the public. The Spanish Colonial-style **Plymouth Congregational Church** on Devon Road is one of the most picturesque in Florida. The building's stones were all cut and set by hand in 1916. The fine door, over 300 years old, comes from a monastery in the Pyrenees. Near by, in a lovely garden setting, is a one-room wooden schoolhouse dating from 1895.

The center of Coconut Grove is the liveliest square in Miami, with street entertainers, European-style sidewalk restaurants and cafés, street markets, corner grocery shops, theaters (most notably the excellent **Playhouse**), and ultra-fashionable night spots. At the **Mayfair Shops** in the Grove Mall, Yves St Laurent and Ralph Lauren boutiques rub designer shoulders with Peter Stringfellow's nightclub, and the brilliant bougainvillaea on the exterior is in lush counterpoint to the sculptures, gleaming exotic tiles and cascading fountains within. In a city famous for its festivals, the Grove is a flag bearer. The big one is the three-day **Arts Festival** in February, which attracts over a million people. The other major festivals are the Bahamian-influenced **King Mango Strut** (late December) and the **Goombay Festival** (June). The best way to discover Coconut Grove is on foot or by bicycle. A novel way of seeing it by two wheels is to board a rickshaw and let a strapping young college type provide the power. If you wish to learn about its history, however, join the free two-hour walking tour conducted by The Villagers, on the last Saturday of each month.

ⓘ Coconut Grove Chamber of Commerce, 2820 McFarlane Road

Continue through Coconut Grove until you reach Le Jeune Road. Turn left here, then right onto Sunset Drive (SW 72nd Street) as far as Red Road (SW 57th Avenue), 4 miles (6km).

Bakery Center

5 A *trompe l'oeil* of man versus alligator welcomes you to the Bakery Center. One of the city's more interesting shopping malls, the third floor features the **Miami Youth Museum**. Unlike many other hands-on discovery centers, here the emphasis is on art rather than science, and youngsters are encouraged to express themselves musically and visually. Return east on Sunset Drive (SW 72nd Street) and turn right (south) onto Old Cutler Road. Drive through the subtropical **Matheson Hammock Park**, 100 acres (40 hectares) of wilderness and mangrove swamp with a delightful man-made beach. At its southern edge is the **Fairchild Tropical Garden**, the largest tropical botanical garden in the US. The collection of

palms here is one of the finest in the world. Other features include a rare-plant house, a tropical rain forest, sunken gardens and a hibiscus garden. A guided tram tour gives an overview of the garden's 83 acres (34 hectares).

Continue a little way and turn right on Red Road (SW 57th Avenue) to **Parrot Jungle**. Established in 1936, this is one of Miami's oldest and best-loved attractions, and even if the bird shows are now looking decidedly dated, you can't help but be impressed by the free-flying birds in this magnificent subtropical jungle. Flamingos, giant banyan trees and delicate orchids complete the visit.

Turn around and head south back down Old Cutler Road and turn right onto Coral Reef Drive (SW 152nd Street) to the Metrozoo, 13 miles (21km).

Metrozoo

6 Hailed as the finest zoo in Florida, Metrozoo provides its residents with a 'natural', largely cage-free environment, where the only thing separating the public from most of the animals is a few feet of space. The stars of the zoo are its splendid rare white Bengal tigers, its lovable koalas (the only ones on permanent display in the US outside California) and its outstanding **Wings of Asia** walk-through tropical aviary. Take the overhead monorail to get a bird's-eye view and give your feet a rest. With over 2,000 animals and a variety of entertaining shows, the zoo makes a great family day out. The **Gold Coast Railroad Museum** (which shares the same site) is more likely to appeal to rail buffs and is a shambling but atmospheric collection of old steam locos recalling the early pioneering days. Go at the weekend when trains are steamed for rides.

Turn left as you leave the site and right (north) onto SW 137th Avenue. **Weeks Air Museum** at the Tamiami Airport is dedicated to some 40 aircraft, from the days of the Wright Brothers to the end of World War II.

Continue north on SW 137th Avenue, turn right at North Kendall Drive (SW 88th Street), cross Florida's Turnpike and turn left (north) onto SR 874 (Don Shula Expressway) until it joins SR 826 (Palmetto Expressway). Head north and turn off right at Coral Way (SW 22nd Street), 19 miles (31km).

Coral Gables

7 Coral Gables is the most exclusive of Miami's many suburbs and, over 70 years after its creation by George Merrick, it still retains its old-world Spanish-Mediterranean ambience. Merrick's house, **Coral Gables House** on Coral Way, is open to the public. Turn right immediately opposite the house, down Toledo Boulevard, to see the most beautiful public swimming pool in Florida. The **Venetian Pool** was carved from coral rock in 1924 and boasts rock caves, stone bridges and a small sand beach, all in a setting worthy of a doge.

Turn right onto Anastasia Avenue. Ahead of you is the architectural *tour*

Above: Ice-cream colors accent the atmosphere of Coconut Grove, an elegant paradise for browsers

Below: A ceremonial Chinese robe, on show at the Lowe Art Museum in Coral Gables

de force of the Gables, the magnificent **Biltmore Hotel**. Just like the downtown Miami Freedom Tower, its central 26-story tower is a 1925 copy of the Giralda in Seville. Turn left before you reach the hotel down Granada Boulevard. You are now heading through the campus of the University of Miami. Turn right at Ponce de León Boulevard, and the excellent **Lowe Art Museum** is on the right, featuring pre-Columbian and Native American art plus exhibits from Asia, Africa and Europe. Make your way back to Ponce de León

Boulevard, follow it around to the left, crossing Bird Road and the Miracle Mile, until you reach SW 8th Street. Just before this street you will see the 40-foot (12m) archway known as the Douglas Entrance, erected in 1924 as the main gateway to Coral Gables.

Continue along SW 8th Street.

Little Havana

8 The area which centers around SW 8th Street (or, in the vernacular, Calle Ocho) is Miami's Latin Quarter. There is little in the way of organized tourist attractions here, but for most visitors the rich tableau of Calle Ocho street life is reward enough. Don't miss the colorful open-air markets with their exotic fruits and vegetables, Havana cigars at Havana prices, old men in their bright *guayaberas* (blousons) playing dominoes, and above all Cuban food—either El Tablao-style (restaurant-nightclub with tableside flamenco) or from a simple sidewalk counter. The classic dish is *arroz con pollo*, chicken cooked in wine and spices and served with yellow rice. Order it accompanied by plantains and black beans.

Follow SW 8th Street back to Brickell Avenue and turn left to Bayside Marketplace, 3 miles (5km).

Bayside Marketplace–Brickell Avenue	1 (2)
Brickell Avenue–Key Biscayne	8 (13)
Key Biscayne–Vizcaya	8 (13)
Vizcaya–Coconut Grove	2 (3)
Coconut Grove–Bakery Center	4 (6)
Bakery Center–Metrozoo	13 (21)
Metrozoo–Coral Gables	19 (31)
Coral Gables–Little Havana	8 (13)
Little Havana–Bayside Marketplace	3 (5)

FOR HISTORY BUFFS

Key Biscayne was named by Ponce de León in 1513 on his first expedition to Florida. His sailors, unaware of the nearby sandbar and submerged reefs, would have much appreciated the **Cape Florida Lighthouse** erected in 1825. Hundreds of vessels have come to grief at this point. Tragedy of a different kind befell the lighthouse itself in 1836, when an attack by Seminole Indians left the lighthouse keeper's assistant dead. The lighthouse is the oldest surviving structure in Greater Miami.

SPECIAL TO . . .

8 *Little Havana* In a city renowned for its festivals, the biggest and most colorful is **Carnaval**, a week of festivities in February or March that dramatically captures the flavor of Little Havana. Around a million people take to the street in boisterous celebrations, so it is not for the faint-hearted. If you want to learn more about the Cuban community, visit the **Cuban Museum of Art and Culture** on Ronald Reagan Avenue (SW 12th Street).

1 day – 78 miles (125km)

GREATER MIAMI NORTH

Bayside Marketplace ● American Police Hall
Morningside Historic District ● Little Haiti
North Miami Beach ● Bal Harbour
Old Spanish Monastery ● Dania
Hialeah Park ● Bayside Marketplace

This short tour of the area floating between the major magnets of Miami and Fort Lauderdale is almost a 'best of the rest'. The places and attractions featured here are hardly off the beaten track, but they are not top priority on most tourist itineraries. En route you will see a little of everyday Miami and South Broward suburbia, but the tour is laced with enough surprises (a 12th-century Spanish monastery), ethnic color (Haitian and American Indian communities) and sporting action (the world's fastest ball game) to satisfy all but the most jaded appetites.

SPECIAL TO . . .

The weekly **Five Star Rodeo** at Davie draws professional cowboys (and cowgirls) from all over the country to compete in thrilling and bruising events such as bronco and bull riding, steer wrestling and calf roping. Daring clowns risk life and limb for laughs, and everyone has a really good time. Don a stetson and go on down to the corner of Davie Road and Orange Drive.

Catching the breeze, a lifeguard surveys the peaceful scene at North Miami Beach, where the atmosphere is simple and unsophisticated

ⓘ Miami North—Greater Miami Convention and Visitors Bureau, Brickell Avenue; South Broward—Greater Fort Lauderdale Convention and Visitors Bureau, Suite 1500, 200 East Las Olas Boulevard

Start at Bayside Marketplace, and head north on Biscayne Boulevard for 3½ miles (5.5km).

American Police Hall of Fame and Museum

1 This unique and fascinating exhibit is a reminder of the seamier side of the city and the national crime problem. Over 10,000 artifacts are displayed, including a mock-up crime scene where you are challenged to 'solve the murder'. The massive marble memorial, which commemorates over 3,000 American police officers slain in the course of duty, is a sobering sight.

Continue north for 1 mile (1.5km). Turn left (west) onto NE 54th Street, then right (north) onto NE 2nd Avenue.

Morningside Historic District

2 This collection of fine Art Deco and Mediterranean Revival homes was built as an early city suburb around 1925. It continues north for five blocks, and some of the larger estates can be seen on the bay front.

Continue north on NE 2nd Avenue for 1 mile (1.5km).

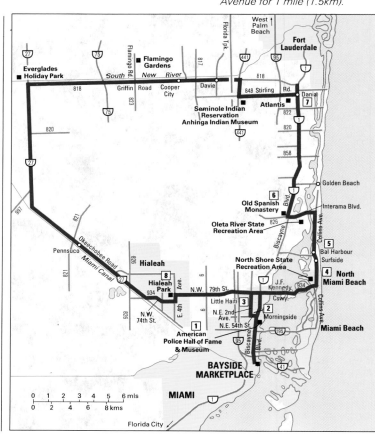

The miles of white sand and the waters of the Atlantic along Miami Beach give the vacationer a sense of limitless space, although high-rise buildings stand near by

Little Haiti

3 A Haitian community 60,000 strong clusters around NE 2nd Avenue. The best place to see their exotic fresh produce and colorful arts and crafts (regarded as the best in the Caribbean) is at the **Caribbean Marketplace** at the intersection with NE 62nd Street. This ethnic enclave continues as far north as the suburb of El Portal, across the Little River (past NE 87th Street).

Turn right (east) onto NW 79th Street, which becomes the John F Kennedy Causeway. Turn left at the beach onto Collins Avenue, 5 miles (8km).

North Miami Beach

4 These shores are much quieter and less sophisticated than those to the south, although the beach around 85th Street is popular with the high school crowd. After the beachside condominiums, the 40-acre (16-hectare) North Shore State Recreation Area, which stretches from 79th to 87th Street, is a welcome oasis of lush tropical vegetation.

Continue north on Collins Avenue for 2 miles (3km).

Bal Harbour

5 A square mile (2.5sq km) of elegance is how Bal Harbour likes to portray itself, and there is certainly no shortage of well-heeled style here. Costly condominiums and a lushly landscaped beach announce Bal Harbour, and the centerpiece is its striking shopping mall, where doyens of international style such as Gucci and Cartier rub shoulders with top American fashion names including Neiman Marcus and Saks Fifth Avenue. The interior setting is a luxuriant tropical garden.

*Continue on Collins Avenue, turn left onto Interama Boulevard (**SR 826**/NE 163rd Street), then right (north) onto **US 1**.*

Old Spanish Monastery

6 The Old Spanish Monastery of St Bernard was originally built in Segovia, Spain, in 1141 and is now said to be the oldest reconstructed building in the Western hemisphere. This beautiful structure was shipped piecemeal to America by the legendary millionaire William Randolph Hearst in 1925, destined for his San Simeon estate in California. After over 20 years in storage, however, it was sold and reassembled here and is now a fitting home to a fine museum of medieval art treasures.

*Continue north on **US 1** (West Dixie Highway) for 9 miles (14.5km).*

RECOMMENDED WALK

Lovely **Oleta River State Recreation Area** stands on the banks of the scenic Oleta River and the Intracoastal Waterway, just off Interama Boulevard (NE 163rd Street). Just a short distance away from the monotonous condominiums and tawdry motels of the northern shores, you can walk, cycle or take a canoe to explore the mangrove forest and surrounding aquatic areas. You will see a good variety of birdlife and small animals and, if you are lucky, dolphins and manatees.

FOR CHILDREN

7 *Dania* **Atlantis: The Water Kingdom**, at Dania, is one of the world's largest water theme parks (check when it is open). Young-at-hearts can have a great day screaming down a seven-story-high water slide, riding the 120-foot (37m) **Raging Rampage** and swirling in the **Wave Pool**. Water skiing and other aquatic performances also take place. Open daily from mid-June to late August; times and days vary in spring and fall.

BACK TO NATURE

Although you may expect to have to travel south to see the Everglades, the northeastern waters of the mighty swamp are just a few miles to the east, behind **US 27. Flamingo Gardens** (on Flamingo Road) will give you a taste of their lush landscape, combining botanic gardens, flamingos and a children's zoo.

Greynolds Park is one of the best bird-watching spots on this tour, and one of the best in Miami as a whole. Scarlet ibises were introduced in 1961 and are occasionally seen among the numerous white ibises. Also look for herons, spoonbills and vultures in abundance.

Dania

7 Entering Dania, you will see many of its 75-plus antique shops along US 1. It is also known for its *jai-alai* (pronounced high-a-lie) *fronton* (stadium). This is the world's fastest-moving ball game, played by two (or four) people on a squash-style court. Using a basket-like glove strapped to the wrist, they catch and hurl a ball at speeds up to 188 mph (303km/h). Although the game itself is an exciting spectacle, betting is a priority for most spectators.

Stirling Road continues west for over 4 miles (6km) past **Atlantis: The Water Kingdom**, as far as **SR 7/US 441**. Visit the **Seminole Indian Reservation** and the **Anhinga Indian Museum and Art Gallery** to learn more about tribal ways.

*Drive north on **US 441**, then turn west through South Broward along Griffin Road **(SR 818)** to see Flamingo Gardens and the Everglades Holiday Park (see **Back to Nature**), then return south to Miami on **US 27**. Turn*

Thoroughbreds parade before taking to the track in Hialeah Park. The park is also home to the world's biggest flock of flamingos

*off left (east) onto **US 934** (NW 74th Street) and head east for 2 miles (3km). Turn left (north) onto East 4th Avenue, 40 miles (64km).*

Hialeah Park

8 This luxuriant 228-acre (92-hectare) park is home to probably the world's most beautiful race track, and certainly to the world's largest flock of some 600 American flamingos. The thoroughbred racing season runs from mid-November to late May, but the park is open for daily tours.

*Take East 25th Street west. This runs into NW 79th Street and after 5½ miles (9km) joins **US 1**. Turn right to head the 4 miles (6km) south back to the Bayside Marketplace.*

Bayside Marketplace–American Police Hall of Fame **3½ (5.5)**
American Police Hall of Fame–Morningside Historic District **1½ (2.5)**
Morningside Historic District–Little Haiti **1 (1.5)**
Little Haiti–North Miami Beach **5 (8)**
North Miami Beach–Bal Harbour **2 (3)**
Bal Harbour–Old Spanish Monastery **5 (8)**
Old Spanish Monastery–Dania **9 (14.5)**
Dania–Hialeah Park **40 (64)**
Hialeah Park–Bayside Marketplace **11 (18)**

Cape Florida Lighthouse, the oldest building in southern Florida, was erected at Key Biscayne in 1825 as a warning for sailors. Submerged reefs make this stretch of coastline treacherous for shipping

*From Bayside take **I-95/US 1** south for 22 miles (35km) and turn right (west) onto Hainlin Mill Drive (SW 216th Street).*

Homestead

1 At **Monkey Jungle** over 50 species of chattering primates run free around 30 acres (12 hectares) of dense jungle, while the humans are caged within protective walkways. The shows here are excellent and star King, the mighty gorilla. Continue west, turn left on to Krome Avenue (SW 177th Avenue), then right (west) onto Coconut Palm Drive (SW 248th Street). The **Redland Fruit and Spice Park** is a unique botanical garden growing over 500 kinds of fruit, vegetables, herbs, spices and nuts. Take a 'fruit safari', then make a selection from the bountiful gourmet and fruit store. Return east and turn right onto Newton Road (SW 157th Avenue). **Orchid Jungle** is the world's largest outdoor orchid garden, with over 9,000 varieties. The cloning laboratory is particularly interesting.

Continue south to the South Dixie Highway (**US 1**) and turn left (east) onto Biscayne Drive (SW 288th Street), where you will see **Coral Castle**. This unique achievement of coral sculptures and buildings was created singlehandedly by Edward Leedskalnin between 1920 and 1940. Its 1,000 US tons (907 metric tons) of coral carving includes a 9-US-ton (8-metric-ton) gate pivoted so that a child can open it, a 28-US-ton (25-metric-ton) obelisk and huge coral rocking chairs. How did he create such sculptures and move such huge weights without machinery, and what was his motivation? 'America's Stonehenge' is as mind-boggling as the real thing. Head north on **US 1** and turn off at Cauley Square, a renovated 1904 railroad village that now houses themed restaurants and shops.

Return south to Coral Castle, go east (left) on Biscayne Drive, turn right (south) onto Tallahassee Road, then left (east) onto North Canal Drive (SW 328th Street).

Biscayne National Park

2 As 96 percent of this park is submerged, the only way to see it is by boat. Excursions vary seasonally, but ranger-guided walks and canoe trips are usually available. The glass-bottom boat voyage to the offshore coral reef is a must. Take along your snorkel to view the teeming sea life.

☒ Convoy Point Information Station and Park Headquarters

Return west on North Canal Drive, turn left (south) on Tallahassee Road (SW 137th Avenue) and right onto Palm Drive (SW 344th Street). Continue for 1½ miles (2.5km) to the intersection with Tower Road/Old 27 (SW 192nd Avenue), where the colorful 'Robert Is

SEA OF GRASS

Bayside Marketplace ● Homestead Biscayne National Park ● John Hudson's Airboats Everglades National Park Main Visitor Center Royal Palm Visitor Center ● Flamingo Bayside Marketplace

It is a great paradox that although nearly every visitor to southern Florida would like to see the Everglades, few have any idea what the area has in store for them. A short drive along the Tamiami Trail leads right into the center of this vast wilderness, past several airboat operators, all ready with an exciting ride and nature tour, to show you 'the real Everglades'. Don't miss an airboat tour, but don't think either that this is what the Everglades are all about. Unspoiled natural serenity is really the essence of the Everglades, and this can be found in abundance on the road to Flamingo and at Shark Valley. Above all, don't be disappointed at first sight. There really is more here than meets the eye, and there are plenty of very willing and able park rangers to help you find it. The first tour passes through the major attractions of Homestead, including the often overlooked Biscayne National Park. (The southwest section of the Everglades is covered in the tour on page 23.)

Here' fruit stall stands. Turn down Tower Road and continue straight on past the junction with SW 376th Street.

John Hudson's Airboats

3 There are more sophisticated and much quieter airboat rides available, but for a real backwoods setting and atmosphere this is one of the best. If you have a choice, opt for the 10-seat 'aircat' —the original style of airboat, with a propeller driven by a powerful auto or aircraft engine, which rips across the saw grass at up to 60 mph (95km/h). With passengers sitting just inches above the water,

---

RECOMMENDED WALKS

All the walks off the road to Flamingo have something special to show visitors, and most are quite short. The **Anhinga Trail** is the best of all for a general overview. The **Pa-Hay-Okee** features an elevated observation tower; at **Mahogany Hammock** you can see the largest living mahogany tree in the US; and at **West Lake** is a fine example of a mangrove forest.

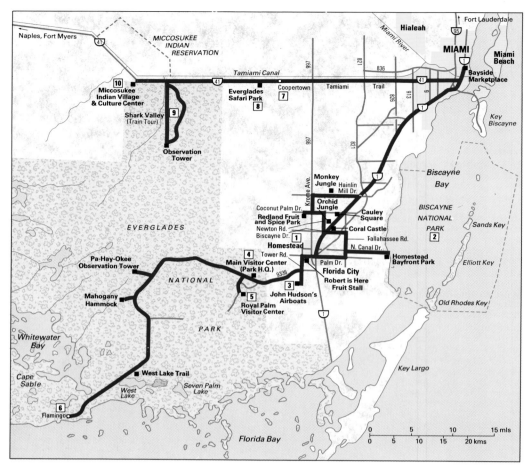

FOR HISTORY BUFFS

The Miccosukee Indians who live around the Tamiami Trail and Alligator Alley are descendants of the Creeks who migrated to Florida in the 18th and 19th centuries and became known as Seminoles—meaning 'wild runaways'. Clashes with settlers and the US army led, in 1818, to the first of the Seminole Wars. Determined to resist the white man's land-grabbing and deportation orders, the Seminoles carried out a bitter guerilla war led by Chief Osceola. After Osceola's capture and death, Billy Bowlegs (who actually had no such deformity) led the surviving band of around 150 Seminoles deep into the Everglades. To this day they have never acceded to the government's treaties.

SCENIC ROUTES

The whole 36-mile (58km) drive from the main entrance of the national park to Flamingo is recommended. Drive slowly to take it in and try to spot the changing ecosystems. You will start in saw grass prairie, pass through pinelands, then cypress forest, hardwood hammocks, mangroves and coastal prairie before reaching the Florida Bay estuary at Flamingo.

the speed sensation is a real thrill. Earplugs (supplied) dull the roar of the engine, but when the boat stops, peace returns and the knowledgeable captain will point out the prevailing wildlife.

*Return north on Tower Road and turn left onto **SR 9336**, 9 miles (14.5km).*

Everglades National Park Main Visitor Center

4 Stop at the Main Visitor Center for an introductory film and to see what ranger-conducted activities are scheduled for that day (look also in the visitor's guide you get at the park entrance). This will include informal introductory talks, walks along nearby trails and a campfire get-together.

A short distance away is the Royal Palm Visitor Center.

Royal Palm Visitor Center

5 Another well-stocked visitor center, plus two of the park's most popular trails, are located here. On the ½-mile (800m) **Anhinga Trail**, alligators, turtles, and several species of fish and birds reside below the boardwalks that cross the slough (water hole). The **Gumbo-Limbo Trail**, also half-a-mile (800m), will introduce you to a hardwood hammock.

*From here the road continues for 38 miles (61km) to Flamingo with turn-offs only to more boardwalks and points of sightseeing interest (see **Recommended Walks**).*

Flamingo

6 This small settlement is basically a staging post for Everglades explorers, with a visitor information center and a small museum relating to the 'glades. Aside from camping, the only place to stay in the national park is the Flamingo Lodge, so booking is essential; *tel:* (305) 253-2241. You can board the **Wilderness Tram** (November to April) during the day, then catch one of the two sunset delights here. The first is a walk around **Eco Pond**, where hundreds of roosting wading birds can be seen flying in at dusk (egrets, herons, ospreys, ibises and red-shouldered hawks are present throughout the day). The second is a romantic bay cruise. There are several charters from the marina, and trips out to **Whitewater Bay** and **Cape Sable** are recommended.

*Return to Homestead, then take **US 1** back to Bayside, Miami, 75 miles (120km).*

A boldly painted totem pole, erected as a symbol of the Miccosukee Indian tribe's identity

From Miami Bayside head south on Brickell Avenue, then west on the Tamiami Trail (also known as Calle Ocho, SW 8th Street or US 41), 23 miles (37km).

Coopertown

7 This small settlement's claim to fame is that the Everglades sequences for the film *Invasion USA* (starring Chuck Norris) were filmed here. Here also are the Everglades airboat tours nearest to Miami.

Continue west along US 41 for 3 miles (5km).

Everglades Safari Park

8 This new, well-run attraction offers a good-value Everglades package of airboat tour, alligator wrestling and tropical jungle trail. The Miccosukee Village, a little further on, has more authentic color.

Continue west along US 41, then turn south (following signs), 14 miles (23km).

Shark Valley

9 Pick up on what's happening daily at the information center before going on the 15-mile (24km) loop to see one of the best concentrations of wildlife in the whole of Everglades National Park. Tram tours lasting two hours cover the area; bike rental is another option (no cars allowed). In winter it is best to book ahead for the tram tour; *tel:* (305) 221-8455. At the tour's southernmost point there is a 50-foot (15m) high observation tower from which to view the vast area of wetlands.

Return to US 41, and turn left to Miccosukee Indian Village, 6 miles (10km).

Miccosukee Indian Village and Culture Center

10 The Miccosukee tribe, hunters and farmers by tradition, has turned part of this village into a tourist attraction featuring craft and cookery demonstrations, alligator wrestling and a small museum. A 40-minute

1 day — 86 miles (139km)

THE TAMIAMI TRAIL

Bayside Marketplace ● Coopertown Everglades Safari Park ● Shark Valley Miccosukee Indian Village Bayside Marketplace

This is a day's trip from Miami to the Everglades, departing and returning along the Tamiami Trail (there is no accommodation along the route). Look in the ditches beside the road for herons, egrets and limpkins. Snail kites are sometimes seen quartering the wetlands beyond.

airboat ride will show you an old Indian camp.

Return to Bayside, Miami, east on US 41, 40 miles (64km).

Bayside Marketplace–Coopertown **23 (37)**
Coopertown–Everglades Safari Park **3 (5)**
Everglades Safari Park–Shark Valley **14 (23)**
Shark Valley–Miccosukee Indian Village **6 (10)**
Miccosukee Indian Village–Bayside Marketplace **40 (64)**

A mass of reptilian muscle looking deceptively docile during a bout of alligator wrestling

FOR CHILDREN

Although children will undoubtedly enjoy Monkey Jungle at Homestead, the shorter and livelier Tamiami Trail is the better of the two Everglades tours for young families. Older children are bound to enjoy a canoe adventure, either at one of the boardwalk trails or with Backcountry Cruises in Flamingo. Because of the mosquito problem, do not take young children to the Everglades in the summer, and carry insect repellent even in winter.

SPECIAL TO . . .

10 *Miccosukee Indian Village* The best time to visit the Miccosukee Indian Village is between Christmas and New Year's Day, when some 40 tribes gather to dance, sing and exhibit at the Florida annual **Indian Arts Festival**.
The **Miccosukee Restaurant** is one of the very few places in Florida where you will get the chance to try American Indian food. Frog's legs, catfish, Indian-style burgers and delicious Indian fry bread and pumpkin bread feature on the menu.

THE EVERGLADES

Exploring the mysterious peace of the Everglades by airboat

The Everglades stretch over 100 miles (160km) south from Lake Okeechobee in the north to Whitewater Bay in the southwest and some 50 miles (80km) east to the start of the Florida Keys. Technically this is a huge river but its flow is imperceptibly slow, and with an average depth of just 6 inches (15cm) it is like no other river in the world. In effect, it is a vast water prairie, or a sea of grass. There are no dramatic contrasts here, no bubbling, muddy swamps beloved of TV adventures, and few tourist attractions. Aside from the thrill of an airboat ride, all is peaceful and calm—the charms of the region are purely natural.

Do not confuse the Everglades with Everglades National Park. The latter is a legally protected, 2,000-square-mile (5,180sq km) area within the former. Its ecosystem is carefully preserved and interpreted for visitors by helpful and knowledgeable park rangers. (Note: airboats are prohibited in the national park.)

PRACTICAL CONSIDERATIONS

Never feed the animals. You risk at best a huge fine, at worst your life. Once an alligator is given food, it loses its fear of man and will subsequently equate all people with food. Alligator attacks are extremely rare, but never approach them too closely as they are deceptively fast and enormously strong. For this reason never swim or wander off on your own in the Everglades. Snakes, too, can be dangerous, though very few are deadly. Don't put your hand or foot under a shady place, such as a rock, without checking first, and be aware of water snakes if you are fishing or canoeing.

Finally, don't let these words to the wise put you off exploring this natural wonderland. As long as you follow the advice given by park rangers before making any independent excursions, there should be no problems.

Wildlife

The Everglades and the American alligator are virtually synonymous. In recent years legal protection has allowed the 'gator to increase its numbers, so that it is now a common sight throughout the area. So, too, is its prey of terrapins and frogs. Crocodiles, recognizable by their tapered snouts, are rare, as is the Florida panther, now reduced to a mere 30 or so, concentrated in the western 'glades and Big Cypress Swamp. However, you may see a 30 to 40-pound (14 to 18kg) bobcat in the pinelands of the national park or around the Flamingo area in the south. Nocturnal raccoons and opossums are common sights around campgrounds. The armadillo is another night creature of the 'glades, most likely to be seen squashed along the roadside. Look out at dawn and dusk for white-tailed deer grazing by the road. Animals that live a partially aquatic existence include the marsh rabbit and the elusive river otter (try Shark Valley for a sighting). The chances of spotting a dolphin in Whitewater Bay and Florida Bay are good, and manatees occasionally visit the Mangrove Wilderness, Everglades City.

Birds

Birdwatchers from all over the world come to the Everglades to view almost 300 species, but there is no need for binoculars to count a good many. Of all these, the species that seem perfectly designed for this watery wilderness are the stately wading birds, often so still (watching for fish) that they appear wooden. Tallest of these, at over 4 feet (1.2m), is the great blue heron. When in its white plumage, it is distinguishable from the slightly smaller great egret by its yellow legs. Other common waders include the little blue heron, the white ibis (red down-curved bill and face mask) and the snowy egret. One of the most popular Everglades sightings is the distinctive bright-pink roseate spoonbill (try Mrazek Pond, near Flamingo, in winter or the shallows off **US 1** just north of Key Largo). A more common sighting is

The alligator is the creature most associated with the Everglades, but you might also spot black bears, sea turtles, otters and raccoons, plus up to 300 types of land and water birds

the anhinga, frequently seen on a tree drying off its outstretched wings. Birds of prey include ospreys, kites and falcons. Soaring overhead, both black and turkey vultures are almost a permanent feature of the 'glades.

The Everglades wilderness owes much of its character to the fact that it was unexplored by white man until the mid-19th century

Flora

The Everglades are, thankfully, not all sharply barbed saw grass, though this is the dominant plant of the region. Small hammocks—raised areas characterized by hardwood vegetation—punctuate the great river of grass, attracting a variety of plant and insect life. This typically includes palms, live oaks, mahogany trees, wild vines and the gumbo-limbo tree (the latter is known colloquially as the 'tourist tree' because in hot weather its bark turns red and peels off). Air plants (bromeliads) thrive in the hammocks by simply attaching themselves to other trees and plants. The most conspicuous of these is the wild pine, which resembles the top leaves of a pineapple, to which it is related. Look out, too, for the bright red of the stiff-leaf wild pine among bald cypress trees. Orchids can be spotted on the Anhinga Trail, but elsewhere these are rare. The national park is the home of the largest mangrove forest in the US. From the elevated boardwalk at West Lake look for good examples of the mangrove's unusual system of above-ground roots.

PRACTICAL CONSIDERATIONS

Winter is by far the best time to visit the area. Birds and animals become more visible as they gather around the receding sloughs (water holes), and the infuriating mosquitoes are virtually absent between January and March. These are a real problem from May to November, even with the protection of a strong insect repellent. If you must go then, cover up well and still expect to be bitten. The only place to avoid them is on the airboats, as the wind prevents them from settling. To appreciate the area fully, you must leave your car and either walk, cycle or, best of all, canoe along ranger-recommended routes. Drive slowly at night to avoid killing small animals.

2 days – 324 miles (520km)

ALONG THE CORAL KEYS

**Miami ● North Key Largo
John Pennekamp Coral Reef State Park
The African Queen/Tavernier ● Islamorada
Marathon and the Middle Keys
The Lower Keys ● Miami**

The popular image of the Florida Keys—coral islands with palm-fringed beaches catering for bronzed hedonists—is an oversimplification. The islands are simply the high points of what was Florida's southern mainland before flooding occurred millions of years ago. However, the largest living coral reef in the Western hemisphere is located just off the Keys, and it is thanks to this that Key Largo has become the diving capital of the world and Islamorada the sportfishing capital. The disadvantage of the reef is that the water along the shore is often too shallow for swimming and, because wave action is sorely limited, fine-sand beaches are very scarce. For the majority of visitors, however, the marvelous underwater opportunities outweigh lying on a beach, and most underwater locations of interest, whether reef or wreck, are accessible to snorkelers as well as scuba divers. Key Largo is lively, Key West (covered separately) can be hectic, but for the most part the Keys are quiet island retreats.

FOR CHILDREN

The Florida Keys are primarily an adult playground for divers and anglers. Older children who want to pick up a rod or use a snorkel are well catered for, but attractions for youngsters are limited. Key Largo is the best area to keep children amused, and on adjacent Windley Key the **Theater of the Sea** is a perennial family favorite.

SCENIC ROUTES

There are 42 bridges between the mainland and Key West, and each gives constantly changing views of beach, sea and the scattered isles. The finest of these is the **New Seven Mile Bridge**, which is an unsurpassed vantage point for taking in the sheer sweep of the Straits of Florida and the Gulf of Mexico. It also gives a fine view of the Old Seven Mile Bridge.

*From Miami take **I-95/US 1** south. Some 3½ miles (5.5km) past downtown Homestead, turn left on Card Sound Road. Cross the toll bridge to Key Largo. Note the mile marker stones along the length of **US 1**. These start at **MM 127** just south of Florida City and finish at **MM 0** at Key West (on this route the first mile marker you will see is **MM 105**).*

North Key Largo

1 This is the wildest place in the Keys. The area immediately across the bridge is part of the **Crocodile Lake Wildlife Refuge**. You may well see some of its inhabitants from the roadside, but don't venture too far out. Turn right onto **SR 905** and you will pass through the **Key Largo Hammock**. This large area of West Indian hardwood also has its dangers. Not only are some of the trees here highly toxic, but this is a pick-up and drop-off point for drug smugglers.

Key Largo was immortalized in the 1948 film classic of the same name, starring Humphrey Bogart and Lauren Bacall, and some scenes were shot in the **Caribbean Club** at MM 104. The

Shelling out: shops offer a vast choice of decorative shells for sale

original building unfortunately burned down in the 1950s, but memorabilia in the current club on the same site recall the movie. The **Key Largo Undersea Park** (MM 103.2) offers an introduction to life below the waves. You can take a conducted snorkeling or scuba dive tour, or, if you prefer to keep your feet dry, take a walk below the lagoon.

ℹ Key Largo Welcome Center, **MM 103.4**

John Pennekamp Coral Reef State Park, Key Largo (MM 102.5)

2 If you visit only one underwater park in the Keys, make sure it is this one. The park and the adjacent marine sanctuary boast 650 varieties of tropical fish and some 40 species of coral. There are lots of wrecks to explore, from a Spanish galleon to a World War II freighter sunk by a U-boat. Ships have also been intentionally sunk in recent years to provide diving points of interest, and these also encourage marine life. Another popular feature is a 9-foot (2.7m) bronze statue, 'Christ of the Deep'. See the visitor center, take a glass-bottom boat tour (booking is advisable—*tel:* (800) 344-8175 outside Florida, (800) 432-2871 in Florida, 451-1621 in Key Largo), then get really close to the reef on a snorkeling or scuba tour. If you would prefer to keep dry, there is still plenty to occupy you, including a huge aquarium, nature trails, boats for rent and a good sand beach. **Kimbell's Caribbean Shipwreck Museum** in

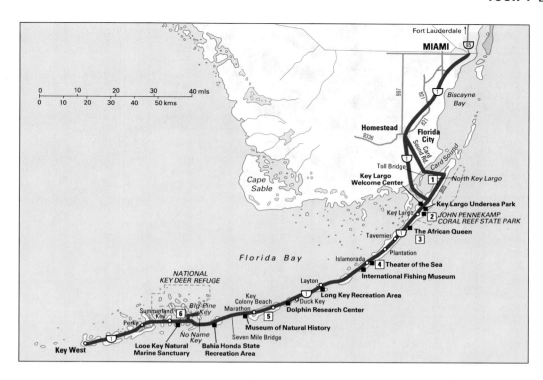

the park exhibits treasures salvaged from local wrecks and from around the world.

The African Queen/Tavernier, Key Largo (MM 100)

3 Another Bogart film legend took its name from a boat, the *African Queen*. Here you will find the original vessel used in the Bogart-Hepburn film, built in 1912 for the African river trade. It is now based on the water at the **Holiday Inn Resort** (MM 100).

Katherine Hepburn provides the link for another vessel here, *Thayer IV*, used for the film *On Golden Pond*, in which she starred alongside Henry Fonda.

Between MM 93 and MM 91 lies the historic town of Tavernier, featuring some of the oldest buildings in the Keys, including an old post office and railroad buildings.

Maritime mecca: yachts at anchor in a Florida Keys marina

BACK TO NATURE

The whole of this trip will delight nature lovers with fauna of West Indian origin, a marvelous concentration of corals and reef life and the delightful Key deer, all unique to the Keys. Drive carefully as many of these tiny creatures are killed by cars.

At the Theater of the Sea, near Islamorada, a dolphin comes ashore to be petted by its trainer

SPECIAL TO ...

You can do just about anything underwater in the Florida Keys. Undersea weddings take place at the statue of *Christ of the Deep* in Pennekamp Park, and honeymooners can even stay below the waves at **Jules' Undersea Lodge** in **Key Largo Undersea Park**. Formerly a research laboratory, this is now the world's first underwater hotel and can accommodate up to six people.

FOR HISTORY BUFFS

Fort Jefferson, located on the **Dry Tortugas** 68 miles (110km) off Key West, is a huge circular Civil War fortress. Its walls are some 50 feet (15m) high, 8 feet (2.4m) thick and guarded by over 140 cannons, yet it has never fired a shot in anger. Visitors must take a boat-trip or seaplane from Key West. The latter gives wonderful views through the shallow waters, including shoals of shark and Mel Fisher's treasure galleon, the *Atocha*.

RECOMMENDED WALK

The geographical distinction of being the southernmost state recreation area means that Bahia Honda has a natural environment that is more Caribbean than North American and is a delightful place for a leisurely stroll. The **Silver Palm Trail** here contains many rare West Indian trees and plants that are not found anywhere else in the Keys.

Islamorada (MM 83)

4 Islamorada (pronounced I-lah-mor-AH-dah) means 'purple isle', possibly named after the purple orchids and bougainvillaea here, and it stretches for 16 miles (26km). The **Theater of the Sea** on Windley Key (MM 84.5) was established in 1946 and has been famous ever since for its performing dolphins. Audience interaction is an important part of its shows. After you have shaken 'hands' with a dolphin, board the glass-bottom boat for a colorful reef tour.

Islamorada is known as the 'Sportfishing Capital of the World', and if you want an introduction to the sport, stop at the **International Fishing Museum**, at Bud 'n' Mary's Marina (MM 79.5). The Keys' latest underwater state park, the **San Pedro**, is also accessible from here.

☐ Islamorada Chamber of Commerce, MM 82.6

Marathon and the Middle Keys (MM 65)

5 More dolphins can be encountered at the **Dolphin Research Center** on Grassey Key, MM 59 (closed Mondays and Tuesdays). There are no shows here—the dolphins are free to come and go at will, though there are some tame residents. The biological diversity of **Crane Point Hammock** (MM 50) makes it the most environmentally important piece of land in the Keys. The **Museum of Natural History** here provides a good insight into the immediate area and the Keys as a whole. At MM 47 is the start of the

Old Seven Mile Bridge, which linked the Middle and the Lower Keys. Destroyed by a hurricane in 1935 and superseded by the New Seven Mile Bridge, it is now the world's longest fishing pier. It is still possible to drive on it as far as Pigeon Key, which is being restored to reflect its days as a railroad camp.

☐ Marathon Chamber of Commerce, MM 49

The Lower Keys (MM 40)

6 The fine mile-long (1.5 km) sandy stretch at the **Bahia Honda** ('deep bay') **State Recreation Area** (MM 37) is the best beach in the Keys. Be careful on **Big Pine Key** to avoid stray Key deer. These beautiful diminutive creatures, measuring just 2 feet (60cm) high, can be seen in the **National Key Deer Refuge** (take Key Deer Boulevard at MM 31.5 to Watson Boulevard).

Continue on to **No Name Key** for even better sightings. If you are searching for solitude, you can find it in many of the outlying Lower Keys, which are uninhabited and barely touched by tourism or the trappings of the 20th century. The reef at **Looe Key National Marine Sanctuary** (MM 27.5), rated by many divers as the most beautiful in the Keys, features many varieties of soft and hard coral and teems with a multitude of sea creatures.

☐ Welcome Center, Big Pine Key, MM 31

Continue to Key West, then return to Miami via **US 1**.

Stripes without stars: the 'Conch Republic' boasts of its latitude on a graffiti-adorned marker buoy

ℹ Key West Welcome Center, North Roosevelt Boulevard; Chamber of Commerce, Mallory Square

Shortly after entering the island, the Overseas Highway (US 1) divides north and south. Turn right (north) onto North Roosevelt Boulevard.

Key West Welcome Center

1 As well as a tourist information center, the Welcome Center is the base for the excellent **Old Town Trolley Tour**, which also operates in Miami (see Tour 1). The long-established and equally fine **Conch Tour Train** (next door) will also welcome you aboard. Both tours last 90 minutes.

Turn around and head south on South Roosevelt Boulevard for just over a mile (1.6km).

Martello Towers and Beaches

2 These twin brick structures were built in the Civil War era as part of the island's defenses. The **East Tower** now houses a comprehensive and lively **museum** and **art gallery**. Drive past **Smathers Beach** to the **West Tower** (closed Mondays and Tuesdays). This also houses an art gallery plus a well-tended tropical garden. Adjacent is **Higgs Memorial Beach**.

Follow the road around to the right as it becomes Reynolds Street. Take the fourth left, South Street. Turn into Whitehead Street, then left, where signed, to Southernmost point.

Southernmost Point

3 A striped marker buoy and plaque confirm that this is the southernmost point in the continental US, just 90 miles (145km) north of Cuba. Just before it you will pass Southernmost Beach and two contenders for the title of Southernmost House. Southernmost shell and coconut vendors ply their wares at this tourist photo-stop, and you will hear conch shells being blown. Pronounced 'konk', the name is applied to the shell, and to its flesh, which features on most south Florida menus.

KEY WEST

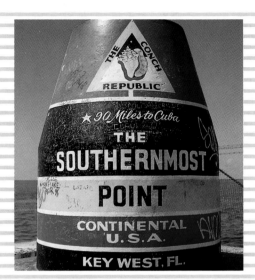

**Key West Welcome Center • Martello Towers
Southernmost Point
Hemingway House • Audubon House
Mel Fisher Maritime Heritage Society Museum
Mallory Square • Duval Street
Caroline Street • City Cemetery
Key West Welcome Center**

There is an incident in the recent history of Key West that captures the essence of its people perfectly. In 1982, in an attempt to catch illegal aliens and drug felons, US police officers set up a roadblock across the Keys, searching every car and asking occupants to prove American citizenship. The people of Key West, outraged at this treatment, rose to the challenge by declaring themselves independent of the US. The 'Conch Republic' was thus formed complete with flag, currency and visas. No sooner had this tongue-in-cheek secession taken place than the roadblock was summarily dismantled.

Within the few blocks that make up the Old Town is one of the biggest concentrations of specialty shops, restaurants, bars and nightlife in Florida. Yet this is also south Florida's oldest city with dozens of beautifully kept historic houses—traditionally weatherboarded, fashioned and fringed with gingerbread grilles in a delightful Bahamian style by ships' carpenters. Hemingway came here and created a hell-raising legend while writing some of America's finest literature. The gentle Audubon was here a century before and produced some of the world's finest art inspired by nature. Key West is like that.

SPECIAL TO . . .

In addition to the nightly performances at Mallory Square, Key West still has plenty of energy to stage festivals. **Old Island Days** is a three-month-long eclectic series of special events highlighting the history, culture and architecture of the island (late January to late March); the **Conch Republic** celebrations in late April–early May recall the island's mock secession; **Hemingway Days** is a week of macho events ending on 'Papa's' birthday, 21 July; **Fantasy Fest**, which embraces Halloween, takes on shades of Mardi Gras and is the wildest of all!

FOR CHILDREN

Although Key West is primarily for adults, there are three marine attractions geared to please children. Both the **Turtle Kraals** and the **Key West Aquarium** have touch tanks where children can feel harmless sea creatures, and both also feature popular heavyweights of the sea—the former quite literally, with its 400-pound (180kg) loggerhead turtles, the latter metaphorically, with a large shark tank. The other show not to miss is **The Wharf Dolphin Show**, where you can watch not only the performance but also how the dolphins actually learn their acts.

FOR HISTORY BUFFS

Fort Zachary Taylor at the western tip of the island is a three-story fort built between 1845 and 1866 to protect the harbor. At the outbreak of the Civil War, it was occupied by Union troops, and although Key West was strongly pro-Southern in its sympathies, the island remained a Union port throughout the war. The fort has recently been designated a state historic site (partly in recognition of its formidable collection of cannons), and there are re-enactments, including a **Massing of the Colors** (part of the Old Island Days festivities).

The beach at Key West may look tranquil, but the area has an unsavory side, having historically been the haunt of characters like smugglers, rum runners and, nowadays, drug dealers

Turn right onto Whitehead Street and head northwest.

Hemingway House

4 No one person is associated more with the island than Ernest Hemingway. The hard-drinking, big-game-hunting, Nobel Prize-winning author bought this elegant Spanish Colonial mansion (built 1851) for $8,000 in 1931. He lived here until 1940 and wrote from his 'tree-house' study *A Farewell to Arms, For Whom the Bell Tolls* and *To Have and Have Not*. Some 40 or so cats live in the house, many of them descendants of 'Papa's' own six-toed feline companions. Their drinking trough is a former urinal from Sloppy Joe's Bar, and is said to be regarded with much reverence by Hemingway aficionados. Almost opposite is the 92-foot (28m) tall old **Key West Lighthouse**, built in 1847. This and the clapboard keeper's house next door have been turned into a **museum**.

Continue for about ½ mile (0.8km). Leave your car and continue on foot round this part of town.

Audubon House

5 John James Audubon, the artist and naturalist famous for his *Birds of America*, stayed at this lovely house (built 1812) while visiting the island to study its native birds in 1832. The period furnishings and antiques, together with Audubon's delightful drawings and engravings, recall peaceful days in old Key West.

Cross the street.

Mel Fisher Maritime Heritage Society Museum and Truman Annex

6 More a treasure trove than a museum, this glittering collection centers on the wrecks of the Spanish galleon *Atocha* and her sister ship, the *Santa Margarita*, both lost off Key West in 1622. In all, some 47 US tons (52 metric tons) of gold and silver were salvaged by Mel Fisher in 1985. Behind the museum is the **Truman Annex**. This new development on the old site of a navy base includes original Victorian houses, a restaurant in the 1891 **Custom House**, a shopping village, the **Ritz Carlton Hotel** and the **Little White House Museum**. The last recalls President Harry Truman's 1948 conference on the unification of the US armed forces.

Continue along Whitehead Street.

Mallory Square

7 By day the square is a lively jumble of marketplace, shops, galleries, bars, restaurants and tour trollies. Here also are two of the island's four theaters, the **Key West Aquarium** and a small factory making hand-made cigars. Every evening at sunset a bizarre circus ritual is played out against a glorious golden backdrop with jugglers, unicyclists, high-wire walkers, singers, mime artists, perhaps a cat-tamer, an escapologist and even a string quartet.

Whitehead Street runs parallel to Duval Street.

Duval Street and Greene Street

8 Duval is famous for its specialty shopping, art galleries, European-style sidewalk cafés and bars. The most famous of these is **Sloppy Joe's**. Hemingway often drank here and the bar is now a shrine to him. A short stumble away is Greene Street and **Captain Tony's**, which also claims to have been the writer's favorite watering hole. Certainly the atmosphere is more authentic here, with fewer tourists. A little further down Duval Street is the **Oldest House** and **Wreckers' Museum**. Here you can learn the 'rules of wrecking' (salvaging), which was one of the mainstays of the island's economy during the early 19th century. The house was built in 1829 and is worth a visit for its age and antiques alone. For more on nautical disasters, visit the **Shipwreck Museum** located in the Old City Hall (built 1891) on Greene Street.

Duval leads onto Caroline Street.

Caroline Street

9 Enter Caroline Street from Duval (near Sloppy Joe's bar) and the **Milton Curry House** (Curry Mansion) is a few yards ahead. This is the grandest of Key West's many fine historic houses. It was built in 1905 and comprises 22 rooms of period antiques.

Continue onto the old shrimp docks and **Land's End Village**, a collection of quaint shops and restaurants with a rustic atmosphere. The **Turtle Kraals**, where turtles were once landed for meat, are now a marine life sanctuary. Here also is a **Hurricane Museum**, where you can learn about the devastation wreaked on the island in 1919 and 1935.

Return to your car, regain Caroline Street, then turn down Margaret Street opposite the Turtle Kraals and continue for four blocks.

City Cemetery

10 Owing to the difficulty of digging into the coral base of the island, this unusual graveyard is made up of above-ground vaults, laid out almost like a neighborhood in neat rows with street signs. The major memorial here is to the sailors killed in the sinking of the USS *Maine* in Havana in 1898, an act that precipitated the Spanish-American War. The character of Key West can be measured by some of the epitaphs here: 'I told you I was sick' and 'At least I know where he's sleeping tonight' are two favorites. As you leave the cemetery turn right onto Angela Street; on Frances Street, on the left, is the excellent **Haitian Art Gallery**.

Continue on Angela Street until it joins Palm Avenue. Turn right, then left, as this becomes North Roosevelt Boulevard. This continues past the Wharf Dolphin Show back to the Key West Welcome Center.

Key West's picturesque Duval Street is the place to go for authentic local dishes such as conch or Key lime pie – or just for a drink

RECOMMENDED WALKS

The **Pelican Path** is a historic walking trail through the original Old Town, that is, the northwest tip of the island area bounded on the south by Angela Street and on the east by the cemetery. An excellent street map leaflet has been produced to guide visitors along the trail, and blue and yellow pelican street signs confirm directions. The tour takes in over 50 historic houses and sites and will appeal to history buffs. Pick up a free leaflet from the Hospitality House in Mallory Square.

BACK TO NATURE

There is no single large area on this tiny island devoted solely to nature, but the abundance of marine life, seabirds, the prodigious hibiscus and bougainvillaea and the small scale of island development should console nature lovers. There is a small wildlife sanctuary at **Salt Pond** (no visitor facilities) behind Smathers Beach, and the gardens of the **Hemingway House**, the **Audubon House** and the **West Martello Tower** are all very inviting.

Don't forget to look for the famous 'green flash' just as the sun sets. Although it can be seen almost anywhere in the world where there is an expanse of sea, Key West offers great opportunities to see this natural phenomenon.

THE SOUTH WEST

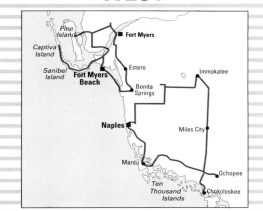

An assembly of anglers congregating on a Sanibel fishing pier

The lighthouse on Sanibel Island

The area between Fort Myers and Naples is known as the Shell Coast, because of the prodigious number of collectible shells that are washed up on its shores. Shelling is a major pastime here and says a lot about what people who choose to visit this part of the state are looking for—serenity, and a simple, natural break. Such a break certainly did no harm at all to Thomas Edison or Henry Ford, who did not actually go shelling, but did come to the area to refresh mind and body—and decades later the world is still reaping the benefits. Expounding on the tourism potential of the region, Edison once prophesied that 'There is only one Fort Myers and 90 million people are going to find it'. Fortunately for the peace of the area, this has never been realized and it is perhaps ironic that the Edison–Ford Complex is now the biggest man-made tourist attraction in southwest Florida. Fort Myers is booming, but it is doing so quietly and if Edison were alive today it is unlikely that he would be displeased (despite his prediction) at how little things have changed in these parts. The region's other attractions are mostly natural, including some of the state's very best wildlife sanctuaries and miles of talcum-white sands dissolving into the blue and green of the Ten Thousand Islands. The name says it all, with apparently thousands of hammocks, in effect mini-jungle islands, scattered along the southwest coast like so much green confetti.

The resorts and cities of the region are generally low-key, and changes brought about by tourism trends are only being felt very gradually. While fashionable travelers flit to and from Miami and the Keys, Naples and Fort Myers welcome back old friends year in, year out, often at a fraction of the prices charged on the Atlantic coast. Few visitors here are short of a dollar, however.

The southwest is acquiring a reputation for attracting some of the country's wealthiest snowbirds, with Naples and Sanibel/Captiva the top destinations. The beautiful Caribbean-like island of Sanibel would be guaranteed a place on any tourist map, regardless of its marvelous shelling opportunities, and fortunately the scale and spacing of development have been sensitively carried out. In general, this is not an area that appeals to teenagers or those looking for 'fun', but for anyone with a more mature view or perhaps feeling a little world-weary, it is a perfect place to relax, recharge the batteries and see a part of Old Florida.

Tour 5

Naples is attractive, wealthy, understated and has miles of pristine sands. For that occasional rainy day the shopping is good, and there are also some fine small museums around the town. Jungle Larry's is a good half-day outing, but to see nature at its best, explore to the east: you will find Corkscrew Swamp and Faka-hatchee Strand as intriguing as their names. Head south to the Everglades to complete your safari. The Ten Thousand Islands and their abundant wildlife are a nature-lover's joy, and the Everglades excursions and trails on this side of the coast are every bit as interest-ing as the more trodden paths into the 'glades from the east coast.

Tour 6

The tour starts at Fort Myers Beach, typical of the miles of unspoiled barrier islands along this coast, yet untypical because of the number of young singles it attracts (this is no Daytona Beach, however). The attractions to the south include the Everglades Wonder Garden, as reliable for a good family outing as its years of experience suggest, and the thought-provoking Koreshan com-munity site. The highlight of the area is the Edison Home—historic house, botanical garden and shrine to one of the century's true geniuses. The restored town center has other attractions, but if you feel like escaping from the madding crowd, then Pine Island is a perfect choice. If this seems too solitary, then the happy medium may be the islands of Sanibel and Captiva, where the beautiful tropical land-scape is truly captivating.

2 days – 138 miles (221km)

NAPLES & THE TEN THOUSAND ISLANDS

**Naples ● Jungle Larry's ● Collier Museum
Corkscrew Swamp Sanctuary
Fakahatchee Strand State Preserve
Ochopee ● Wooten's ● Everglades City
Chokoloskee ● Collier-Seminole State Park
Marco Island ● Naples**

As you enter Naples along the Tamiami Trail, first impressions are not inspiring. However, beyond this neon-lit strip of fast-food joints and faceless malls is a small, well-kept community that has been a highly desirable retirement haven for some years and is just starting to open its doors to an unobtrusive brand of tourism. There is wealth here in abundance. You can see it in the designer shops and manicured neighborhood lawns, but for the best view take a cruise on the scenic finger canals of Port Royal and Gordon Pass. With its picturesque waterways and golden beaches, Naples also possesses natural wealth. It certainly does not flaunt it, however. Much of Naples sprawls in a long thin strip between the Gulf of Mexico and Goodlette-Frank Road, one block east of US 41. The center of town, Old Naples, runs more or less from 1st to 14th Avenue South and clusters around the exclusive shopping district of 3rd Street South. Other focal points are the *City Dock and Yacht Basin* (at the end of 12th Avenue), which is a delightful place to take some waterside refreshment, and the *Old Marine Market-place* at Tin City (at 5th Avenue South). This is a collection of some 40 shops, set along cobbled and planked riverwalks, housed in old boat sheds and riverside buildings. Nautical antiques abound and there are more waterside eating and drinking opportunities. Several boat tours depart from here, among them the Polynesian-style Tiki Islander craft, which will take you on shelling (shell-gathering), fishing or general sightseeing excursions to the Ten Thousand Islands or along the inland waterways.

Sunset in Naples: 41 miles (66km) of palm-graced public beaches – the city's proudest boast – meet the warm waters of the Gulf of Mexico

ⓘ Naples Area Chamber of Commerce, 1700 N Tamiami Trail

From the 5th Avenue bridge head north on Goodlette-Frank Road (SR 851) for 2 miles (3km).

Jungle Larry's Zoological Park and Caribbean Gardens

1 Jungle Larry's is Naples' main attraction, set in 52 acres (21 hectares) of tropical gardens amid stately banyan trees, rustling palms and towering bamboo. Big cats are a specialty, with lions, tigers, cougars and even a hybrid tiger-lion 'tigon'. Some of these are put through their paces at the animal shows, while feathered performers entertain at the tropical bird circus. Take a safari island cruise to see more exotic inhabitants in near-natural surroundings. Sharing the same site is The Conservancy Naples Nature Center, although this is only accessible from 14th Avenue North. This features a small science exhibit with hands-on displays of the habitats and wildlife of south Florida, a wild animal rehabilitation clinic, plus nature trails.

Continue north and take the next right, Golden Gate Parkway (SR 886). Continue for 1½ miles (2.5km) and turn right onto Airport Pulling Road (SR 31). Take the fifth right, Horseshoe Drive.

Collier Automotive Museum

2 This recently established museum is one of the country's finest collections of classic racing and sports cars. There are some 75 automobiles in all, featuring the best collection of Porsches outside the Porsche company's own museum. There is Gary Cooper's supercharged 1935 Duesenberg, a 1928 Hispano-Suiza (once the most expensive car in Europe), a 1914 Rolls-Royce Silver Ghost and several Grand Prix winners. All the cars are maintained in tip-top running condition.

Return to SR 31 and head north for 7¾ miles (12.5km) to SR 846. Follow this east, then north for 18½ miles (30km).

Corkscrew Swamp Sanctuary

3 This 11,000-acre (4,450-hectare) park takes its name from a twisting creek that flows through it. Here you can see North America's largest surviving stand of virgin bald cypress forest, which includes trees over 500 years old and up to 100 feet (30m) tall. The sanctuary has the largest colony of wood storks in the country, and you might see them nesting in the cypress trees from November through April. Look down from the boardwalk trail and you could also spot alligators or even otters.

At Jungle Larry's the tamer attractions include a petting farm, tram tours and picnic facilities

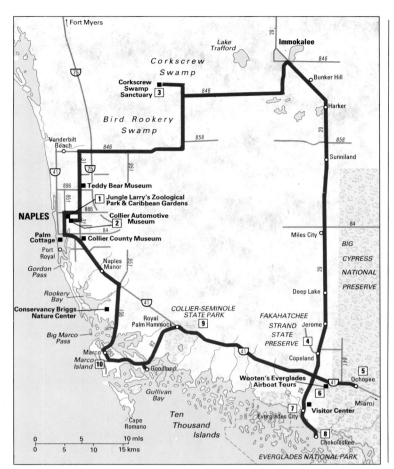

Most of the attractions in this area are natural and feature excellent boardwalk trails. These are pleasant only in the winter, however, due to the presence of infuriating mosquitoes at other times of the year. You should also take a stroll along the beach, keeping one eye open for some of the exotic shells this whole coast is famous for.

FOR HISTORY BUFFS

Naples The **Collier County Museum**, 2 miles (3km) south of the center of Naples on **US 41**, traces the history of the county from pre-historic times to the present. A 2-acre (0.8-hectare) historical park takes a look at a Seminole village and also features a steam locomotive. For history *in situ*, see the **Palm Cottage** at 137 12th Avenue South. This 12-room house built in 1895 is one of the last homes in southwest Florida built of tabby (an ancient shell-and-sand concrete mixture).

SCENIC ROUTES

The most scenic routes in this region can be seen only from the water. However, the southern end of **SR 29** alongside **Big Cypress National Preserve** is pleasant and spiced with the added possibility (however slim) of catching sight of the elusive Florida panther. At the very southern end of this road you will see tall palms, houses on stilts and a countryside little touched by tourism.

Corkscrew Swamp Sanctuary, a huge wilderness area maintained by the National Audubon Society, is home to a number of threatened species, including the Florida panther and the bald eagle. There is a 2-mile (3km) self-guiding tour along elevated boardwalks, so allow at least an hour or two to see the plant and animal life in the surrounding area

Continue east for approximately 10 miles (16km) on SR 846. At Immokalee head due south on SR 29 for 31 miles (50km) to Copeland.

Fakahatchee Strand State Preserve

4 Fakahatchee Strand is the major southwestern drainage channel of the aptly named Big Cypress Swamp.

The vegetation here is outstanding, with the largest forest of native royal palms and the largest concentration and variety of epiphytic orchids in North America. Endangered wildlife includes the wood stork, the Florida black bear, the Everglades mink and the Florida panther.

Continue south for 3 miles (5km) and turn left onto US 41. Head east for 4 miles (6km).

Ochopee

5 This tiny village's claim to fame is that it operates the smallest **post office** in the US. The simple wooden one-person shack measures just over 7 feet by 8 feet (2.1m by 2.4m). Send yourself a postcard from here to get its unique postmark!

Head back west on US 41 for 2 miles (3km).

Wooten's Everglades Airboat Tours

6 Wooten's is something of an evergreen in the 'glades, having operated here since 1953. It also claims to run the only tours that cover grasslands, mangroves and the Ten Thousand Islands. The airboats will take you on a fascinating 5-mile (8km) tour along the old Indian canoe trails used during the Seminole Wars and also into the mangrove jungles on the west coast. The firm also operates swamp buggies, which resemble the metal skeleton of a double-decker bus with huge tires for squelching through the wet terrain (seats are on the top deck only). These venture out to **Halfway Creek Cypress Swamp**, its waters stained a ruddy brown by the tannin from the mangroves where air plants and orchids flourish. To complete your visit see the alligator farm containing some 200 residents and a collection of other Florida reptiles.

Head west for 2 miles (3km) on US 41 and turn left on SR 29 to enter Everglades National Park. Stop at the visitor center to pick up information. Continue south for 4 miles (6km).

Everglades City

7 This small community is the embarkation point for Ten Thousand Islands trips and various sportfishing excursions. There are several companies offering various packages of boat or airboat tours combined with alligator farms, small zoos and even a Miccosukee Seminole Indian village. All of these provide good value for money, but for the most authoritative trip aboard a quiet boat that will not have the indigenous wildlife scooting for cover, go to the National Park Information Center. The park's boats (some are double-decked) glide silently around the Ten Thousand Islands and, on the longer cruises, stop for shelling on a deserted key.

If you plan to stay overnight here, there are two outstanding resorts that are certainly worth seeing, if only for a drink. The **Port of the Islands**, considered one of the finest sportsmen's lodges in the country, is an attractive place in its own right, with a

chickee (Indian palm hut) waterfront bar overlooking a manatee sanctuary. The **Everglades Rod and Gun Lodge** is an even more famous sportsmen's retreat and has played host to a number of shootin' 'n' fishin' US Presidents. Built in the mid-1800s and remodeled in 1920, it is well worth a look and perhaps a meal.

Continue on SR 29 for 4 miles (6km).

Chokoloskee

8 Take the second right past the Chokoloskee post office, then the first left to the historic **Smallwood Store**, perched above the water on stilts. This old Indian trading post and general store was built in 1906 by Ted Smallwood, who traded furs, turtles and venison with the Seminoles. Little has changed since those days except that the store is now a museum.

Return through Everglades City and turn left onto US 41. Continue west for 16 miles (26km).

Collier-Seminole State Park

9 To the right as you enter the park is a skeletal metal wheeled contraption, a 'walking dredge' used to construct the Tamiami Trail in the 1920s. The building a little further on to the left is a replica of a blockhouse used by US forces and local defenders during some of the final skirmishes of the Second Seminole War (late 1850s). Like the Fakahatchee Strand this park is also blessed with abundant stately royal palms and many endangered animal species. You can go on a ranger-guided tour along the nature trail, take to the water on a 13-mile (22km) canoe trip, or go the easy way, aboard the 38-foot (11.6m) *Seminole Princess*.

Head south on SR 92 for 4 miles (6km).

Marco Island

10 Turn left immediately after the bridge onto the island to the small fishing village of **Goodland**. Happily, very little of the modern construction that has completely obliterated the rest of the island's character has reached Goodland. Shops, restaurants and old homes, many on stilts, look peacefully out onto the water.

Return to SR 92, turn left to reach the center of the island, then turn right onto SR 951. Head north for 8 miles (13km) to rejoin US 41, which will take you back to Naples, 5th Avenue South (7 miles/11km).

Naples–Jungle Larry's **2 (3)**
Jungle Larry's–Collier Museum **3 (5)**
Collier Museum–Corkscrew Swamp **27 (43)**
Corkscrew Swamp–Fakahatchee **41 (66)**
Fakahatchee–Ochopee **7 (11)**
Ochopee–Wooten's **2 (3)**
Wooten's–Everglades City **6 (10)**
Everglades City–Chokoloskee **4 (6)**
Chokoloskee–Collier-Seminole **24 (39)**
Collier-Seminole–Marco Island **4 (6)**
Marco Island–Naples **18 (29)**

FOR CHILDREN

Naples **Frannie's Teddy Bear Museum** in Naples claims the most comprehensive collection of teddy bears in America. Here, in a cottage in the woods on Pine Ridge Road (3 miles/5km due north of the Collier Automotive Museum), children will find tough teds in overalls and boots, chintz and cashmere bears, ursa majors measuring up to 6 feet (1.83m) and ursa minors that are just 1 inch (2.5cm) tall. Antiques from the likes of Steiff rub furry shoulders with bears belonging to famous celebrities, and there is a display of bear memorabilia including a signed first edition of *Winnie The Pooh*.

SPECIAL TO ...

As you drive south along **SR 29**, signs announce that you are '**Entering Panther Habitat**' and '**Panther Crossing Next 5 Miles**'. There is certainly no reason to be alarmed, but do take your foot off the accelerator a little on the very remote chance that one of these handsome beasts may grace you with its presence. Depletion of its natural habitat has reduced the population to around 30 in the whole of the eastern United States; nonetheless, relatively frequent panther sightings are made on the 4-mile (6km) stretch between Ochopee and SR 29.

BACK TO NATURE

Naples Much of this tour is devoted to attractions and areas that are completely natural. However, the **Conservancy Center** at Naples has a sister operation, the **Conservancy Briggs Nature Center** (at Rookery Bay National Estuarine Research Reserve), which is particularly appealing to bird-watchers. An elevated walkway winds through pinewoods, scrub oak, salt marsh and mangrove communities. At the midway point an observation platform overlooks a coastal pond where wood storks, great blue herons, snowy egrets and red-breasted mergansers come to feed.

1/2 days – 139 miles (223km)

LEE ISLAND COAST

Fort Myers Beach ● Everglades Wonder Gardens
Koreshan State Historic Site
Edison-Ford Complex ● Fort Myers Historical Museum
Fort Myers Yacht Basin ● Shell Factory
Pine Island ● Sanibel and Captiva Island
Fort Myers Beach

Apart from the Everglades, the Lee Island Coast is the least developed part of southern Florida. Peace and solitude are easy to find on Pine Island and its neighbors, many of which are still undisturbed and scarcely inhabited. The resort of Fort Myers Beach is situated at the northern end of Estero Island, a 7 mile (11km) stretch of white sandy shores and a favorite spot for shelling. This is the liveliest of the Lee Island resorts, popular with young singles and families attracted by the gently shelving beach and the absence of riptides or undercurrents. In addition to the usual amenities, you can cruise across the tranquil bay to admire the waterfront homes, see the occasional dolphin and meander around the mangrove islands. Nature lovers will enjoy *Matanzas Pass Preserve*, a serene refuge of mangroves, gumbo-limbos and cabbage palms inhabited by ospreys and woodpeckers. At the southern end of the island, a tram leads from *Carl E Johnson Recreation Area* to *Lover's Key*, one of the area's favorite beaches.

We sell seashells by the seashore: the Fort Myers area is renowned for hundreds of types of shells

🄸 Greater Fort Myers Beach Chamber of Commerce, 1365 Hendry Street

*Head south for 14 miles (23km) on **SR 865**, through Lover's Key and Big Hickory Island. At Bonita Beach turn inland through Bonita Shores. Three miles (5km) past the latter, turn left onto **Old US 41 (SR 887)**.*

Everglades Wonder Gardens

1 This small lush garden zoo is southwest Florida's oldest attraction and, in places, could do with a coat of paint. However, the low admission price and the enthusiastic guides more than make up for any aesthetic shortcomings with an entertaining and educational tour of the gardens' residents.

Among the many mammals, birds and reptiles, Big Joe the crocodile is king at 1,000 pounds (450kg), but the playful Everglades river otters are the show-stealers.

*Head north to join the Tamiami Trail **(US 41)** and continue for 5 miles (8km).*

Koreshan State Historic Site

2 In 1894 a religious visionary named Cyrus Reed Teed (who gave himself the biblical name Koresh) brought his followers from Chicago to a place he named Estero. His belief that the earth was a hollow sphere with the sun in the center and that he was immortal were two of his more fanciful theories. His teachings advocated celibacy, communal living and communal ownership of property. The community and movement declined after his death in 1908, but you can take a guided tour to see the tropical gardens and several buildings (cottages, workshops, store, etc) that have been restored to their turn-of-the-century appearance.

Busy fishing on Sanibel pier; for a change of pace pedal a rented bicycle along paved trails beneath a green canopy of trees

Continue north for 12 miles (20km) on **US 41** and turn left onto Colonial Boulevard to reach McGregor Boulevard. Follow this road north for nearly 3 miles (5km).

Edison-Ford Complex

3 Fort Myers is indelibly stamped with the genius of Thomas Alva Edison. Even McGregor Boulevard is a tribute to him, for it was he who first planted the stately royal palms that line 15 miles (24km) of road here, hence Fort Myers' nickname, 'City of Palms'. Edison was the most prolific inventor the world has ever seen, and in total he patented 1,300 inventions, the best-known being the electric light bulb and the phonograph. His major achievement while at Fort Myers, which he made his winter home at the age of 38 in 1886, was the development of rubber from the goldenrod plant. The chemical lab in which he pioneered the modern synthetic rubber industry is perhaps the highlight of the tour, appearing today exactly as he left it, with the original light bulbs still going strong after all these decades! The 14-acre (6-hectare) tropical garden is one of the most complete in America and contains over a thousand plant varieties brought from all over the world for experimental purposes. King of them all is the incredible banyan, which Harvey Firestone brought here in 1925 as a sapling with a mere 2-inch (5cm) diameter. It now shades the whole parking lot; with a circumference of 400 feet (122m) it is the second biggest in the world.

Henry Ford, who for a long time had been a close business associate and friend of Edison's, built his winter home next door in 1916. You can see the Model T that Ford gave Edison in 1907, still in running condition and

Fort Myers Historical Museum focuses on local Indian culture, Spanish exploration and early settlers

with a goldenrod rubber spare tire. Despite being the world's first billionaire, Ford had modest tastes and his house is extremely pleasant without ever being grand. A **museum** is dedicated to his achievements during his 15 winters here. After Edison's death in 1931, Ford did not return to Fort Myers. (In order to catch the tours of both homes arrive by 3 pm.)

As you leave the parking lot follow the signs to the Fort Myers Historical Museum, a few blocks east.

Fort Myers Historical Museum

4 Housed in the 1924 Atlantic Coastline Railroad Depot, this is a local and regional museum. Hear in their own words the stories of different generations of local Indians, see models of early Fort Myers and admire the fine glass collection. Outside the museum is **The Esperanza**, the last and the largest Pullman private railroad car to be built. Your guide will show you aboard and take you back to the days of 1929.

Head north on Jackson Street for about 1 mile (2km) and park.

Fort Myers Yacht Basin and Downtown

5 This busy focal point offers several sightseeing tours, including an **Everglades Jungle Cruise** and a paddlewheel lunch excursion. It is a good place to have a drink and watch the busy **Caloosahatchee** ('river of the Calusa Indians'). First Street, one block back, runs through the middle of downtown, where there are

BACK TO NATURE

Fort Myers Well away from the main route (20 miles/32km north of Fort Myers on **SR 31**) is the **Babcock Wilderness Adventure**. A large elevated jeep-like swamp buggy will take you on a 90-minute journey into the beautiful forests and waters of this unspoiled backwoods. Knowledgeable tour guides will point out the abundant wildlife and tell you about life on the range. Seats must be reserved in advance; *phone:* (813) 656-6104.

8 *Sanibel Island* The 'Ding' Darling Wildlife Refuge on Sanibel is a must.

FOR HISTORY BUFFS

3 *Edison-Ford Complex* There are no top-quality historical museums on this route, but the collection in the **Edison Museum** is not only a tribute to the genius of one man, it is a series of landmarks in 20th-century technological breakthroughs. Here you can see some of the world's earliest lighting, phonographic, cinematic and telegraphic equipment, as well as the more mundane domestic prototypes of electric fans, toasters, heaters, water softeners and much, much more.

several restored old-style shopping arcades and squares. Walk east three blocks and on the corner of Fowler Street you will see the splendid **Burroughs House**, completed in 1901. Just renovated, the house may be open to visitors (ask at the Chamber of Commerce) but is worth a look from the outside in any case.

🛈 Fort Myers Chamber of Commerce, Hall of 50 States, 1365 Hendry Street; Lee County Visitors and Convention Bureau, 2180 West First Street

*Cross the river on **US 41** and continue north for 5 miles (8km).*

Shell Factory

6 This 50-year-old tourist institution, spread over a massive 65,000 square feet (600sq m), claims the biggest selection of shells and coral for sale in the world. Tasteful it isn't, but for sheer scale and choice of merchandise (which includes foods, 'fashion items' and tourist trinkets) the place has a fascination all its own. Bouncy water boats and various children's amusements are also on site.

*Return south for 1½ miles (2km) and turn right onto **SR 78**. Head west for 13 miles (21km) to Matlacha, stop at the Pine Island Chamber of Commerce, then continue for a further 4 miles (6km) to Pine Island.*

Pine Island

7 There are no tourist attractions or towering hotels on this sparsely populated barrier island, but if you want to see a little of the old Florida, then the hamlet of **Bokeelia** (turn

right and go to the end of the island) is as good a place as any. Wander out on one of the fishing jetties, perhaps cast a line, watch the pelicans wheeling and diving, enjoy a seafood meal in the simple home-style restaurant and you have exhausted most of the leisure options here. You can rent a boat to one of the other islands —**Useppa, Cabbage Key** or perhaps Lacosta—where you will find life little different. The latter island is home to **Cayo Costa State Park**, where the bird life is spectacular. Lacosta is also one of the few places in North America where mangoes are successfully cultivated. You don't have to go there to enjoy them, however, as they are sold at the friendly roadside stall at **Pine Island Center**, just as you enter the island.

Return via Matlacha. Four miles (6km) after rejoining the mainland, turn right on Chiquita Boulevard. Follow this south to Cape Coral Boulevard, turn left and follow the road for 4 miles (6km) to Cape Coral Bridge, which crosses the Caloosahatchee, onto McGregor Boulevard. Head south (right) for 9 miles (14km) to the Sanibel Causeway.

Sanibel and Captiva Island

8 Sanibel Island is world famous for its shell gathering. Its crescent shape, the smooth, gentle slope of the Gulf floor and its protected situation as a barrier island allow even the most fragile shells to be washed up on its shores intact. More varieties can be found here than on any other beach in North America; among the

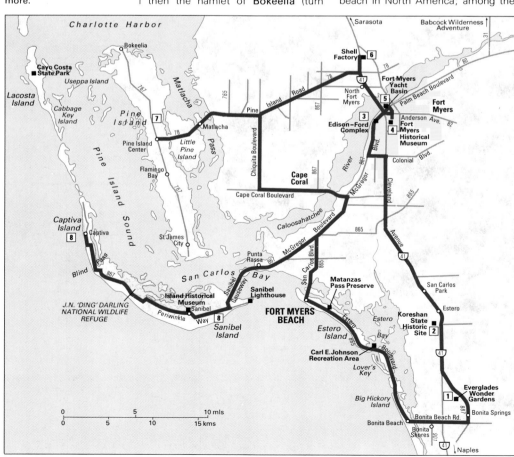

400 types are such exotically named shells as golden tulip, sculpted lion's paw, tiger's eye, lady's ear and angel wings. Pick up a leaflet at the Chamber of Commerce to get started and think about hopping aboard a shelling charter boat, or taking a guided shelling walk (you must also heed the island's regulations on the taking of live shells).

Periwinkle Way is the main road through the 12-mile (19km) length of this island. Turn left on this road just after entering the island to see the **lighthouse**, built in 1884. Turn around and continue for about 4 miles (6km) to visit the **Island Historical Museum**, adjacent to the city hall. Dedicated to the island pioneer families, it contains household furniture and artifacts from the 1900s (open Thursday to Saturday). Close by is the **Schoolhouse Gallery**, housed in a former Baptist church school, built in 1910. The island attracts artists and crafts- people and the gallery has one of the best collections of their work. Con- tinue for 2 miles (3km) and turn right to the **J N 'Ding' Darling National Wildlife Refuge**. This comprises an informative visitor center, a 5-mile (8km) wildlife drive (closed Fridays), two red mangrove forest canoe trails and three walking trails.

From the wildlife drive exit, con- tinue for 2 miles (3km); Captiva Island

Lush vegetation on Sanibel supports an abundance of bird life

begins at **Blind Pass**. The current is strong here, and this is a favorite spot for doing the 'Sanibel Stoop' (as shelling is known here). Captiva is even prettier than Sanibel and hosts some world-class resorts. In this idyl- lic setting it seems that even names such as South Seas Plantation are not overly exaggerated. Drive as far as you can and enjoy your own little piece of American Tahiti on its beautiful northern beach.

ℹ️ Sanibel/Captiva Chamber of Commerce

Return via McGregor Boulevard (SR 867), turning right onto San Carlos Boulevard (SR 865) to Fort Myers Beach.

Fort Myers–Everglades Wonder Gardens **20 (32)**
Everglades Wonder Gardens–Koreshan Site **6 (10)**
Koreshan Site–Edison-Ford Complex **15 (24)**
Edison-Ford Complex–Fort Myers Museum **1 (2)**
Fort Myers Museum–Fort Myers Yacht Basin **1 (2)**
Fort Myers Yacht Basin–Shell Factory **5 (8)**
Shell Factory–Pine Island **18 (29)**
Pine Island–Sanibel/Captiva **28 (45)**
Sanibel/Captiva–Fort Myers **45 (72)**

RECOMMENDED WALKS

Fort Myers City folk may feel more at home exploring old Fort Myers on foot. You can pick up a self-guided tour from the Chamber of Commerce.

8 *Sanibel Island* There are several nature walks on this route but the loveliest are at Sanibel's **'Ding' Darling Wildlife Refuge**. Nearly 2 miles (3.2km) of trails are located at the **Bailey Tract** where alligators, herons and egrets are found, while the 4-mile (6km) **Indigo Trail** enables visitors to see ospreys and wading birds at close quarters.

FOR CHILDREN

Aside from the excellent safe beaches there are not too many obvious places for children on this route. The **Everglades Wonder Gardens** and the **Shell Factory** should entertain the younger ones, and teenagers with inquiring minds will find stimulation, and quite possibly inspiration, at the Edison- Ford Complex.

GOLD COAST & TREASURE COAST

The gold and treasure that these shorelines were originally named after came mostly from the booty of wrecked Spanish galleons during the 17th century. In the late 19th century and early 20th century, the wealth created largely by just two men would have filled several armadas of galleons. The first man was Henry Morrison Flagler, the father of Florida tourism. There was little in the way of charity balls, polo clubs and championship golf courses when his railroad thundered past the yellow wooden shacks of Palm Beach in 1894. Only two years later the legendary Breakers Hotel was accumulating a formidable list of guest signatures, and by the time Flagler had built his great mansion, Whitehall—'The Taj Mahal of North America'—in 1902, Palm Beach was an established mecca for every East Coast socialite. 'Get the big snobs,' as Flagler might have said, 'and the little ones will follow.'

This was, in fact, Addison Mizner's business philosophy, and appropriately the famous architect arrived in Palm Beach in 1925 aboard Flagler's Orange Blossom Special. Mizner turned his attention to the beach resorts to the south and his 'Bastard-Spanish-Moorish-Romanesque-Gothic-Renaissance-Bull Market-Damn the Expense' style (as it was succinctly named) became the hallmark of the area. Perhaps the greatest legacy left behind by this flamboyant character is the Cloister Inn at Boca Raton — a giant pink wonder that remains one of the most costly hotels ever built.

Mizner also knew how to turn a dollar: during the height of the boom, his development company was said to be selling some $2 million worth of real estate per week. Real-estate gold turned to fool's gold with the Great Depression in 1929, but the seeds were sown and Palm Beach County has never really gone out of fashion since. By comparison with these elegant communities, Fort Lauderdale, a fine middle-market family resort, seems at first sight a little vulgar. Behind the souvenirs and bars on the beachfront, however, lie mansions that would not be at all out of place in Palm Beach itself. To the north of Palm Beach is the Treasure Coast. The main attraction for many visitors here is that there are no main attractions — simply peace, quiet, good facilities within easy reach, and miles of golden sand.

City Tour 4

The tour starts in Fort Lauderdale. Nothing remains of the original fort built in 1838 during the Second Seminole War, but there is the settlement's first trading post, now Stranahan House, from which the city grew. The modern concrete development downtown brings you up to date with a jolt before heading to Las Olas Boulevard for some shopping and a foretaste of Worth Avenue in style and price. This is also an indicator of the wealth of Fort Lauderdale; to appreciate this fully, take a river cruise to view the magnificent waterside homes.

Tour 7

North of Fort Lauderdale is the lively suburb of Pompano Beach, where there is plenty to keep all the family amused. Entering Palm Beach County you will encounter Mizner's Boca Raton and its sister resort of Delray Beach, which offers the unusual Japanese Morikami Museum. Next, stop off at Lake Worth for the area's best beach. West Palm Beach is unexpectedly good for children and is also home to the outstanding Norton Gallery of Art. In Palm Beach, stop at Whitehall for a history lesson from the horse's mouth, then padlock your wallet for fabulous Worth Avenue. Continue north through the turtle beaches of Juno and Jupiter and

on to peaceful Hutchinson Island. The road leads back past the scenic Indian River, and the wild and lovely Loxahatchee River in Jonathan Dickinson State Park.

The Henry Morrison Flagler Museum, Palm Beach

Lifeguards patrol Boca Raton Beach with a sharp eye

FORT LAUDERDALE

Bahia-Mar Yacht Center ● Port Everglades
Ocean World ● Museum of Art
Historical Society Museum/Himmarshee Village
Las Olas Boulevard ● Bonnet House
Bahia-Mar Yacht Center

Fort Lauderdale is a lively modern resort with beaches comparable to those of Miami, glittering residences to match Palm Beach, and a well-balanced ambience all its own. It wasn't that way in the 1960s, however, when raucous college students regularly turned the frontage into one big beer-swilling competition. Thankfully, that legacy is now all but gone, though some tacky oceanfront bars remain. Far more typical of the town today are wealthy retirees and young married couples with families. Yet the city retains a buzzing nightlife and is renowned for its choice of eating establishments. At the last count there were 2,500 (excluding fast-food restaurants), with many enjoying a charming waterside location; seafood, of course, is a specialty.

For those with only a day or two to spend in Fort Lauderdale, or who would like a lively introduction to the city sights, then a seat on the *Voyager Sightseeing Train* is recommended. As the tram cars make their way around the 18-mile (29km) loop, passengers learn the history of the town and enjoy anecdotes about the rich and famous who have made their homes here. Close to the Voyager station a competing service, *Lolly the Trolley*, offers free reboarding for a higher initial fare.

SPECIAL TO . . .

For a Fort Lauderdale tour with a difference, take the **Florida Princess Murder Mystery Cruise**. During the course of the evening, a 'murder' occurs, and guests get clues as to 'who dunnit' from the cast of characters who roam the ship. A buffet and live musical entertainment are also provided. The cruise operates on alternate weekend nights only.

ℹ Greater Fort Lauderdale Convention and Visitors Bureau, 500 Broward Boulevard, Suite 104

Start at the Voyager Sightseeing Train Station. Bahia-Mar Yacht Center is adjacent.

Bahia-Mar Yacht Center

1 Bahia-Mar is one of the largest marinas in the country. The front of the dock is always busy, and it is not uncommon to see deep-sea catch —shark, sailfish, or marlin weighing up to 300 pounds (136 kg)—strung up fresh from fishing charter boats. Glass-bottom snorkeling boats are a great way to explore shallower

---

Exotic birds are only part of the entertainment at Ocean World

waters and coral reefs, and an illuminated night excursion is particularly memorable. If your idea of a cruise is passive relaxation, however, there are plenty of conventional sightseeing tours along the inland waterways. The *Jungle Queen* steamboat has been offering family excursions around Fort Lauderdale since 1945. Three-hour daytime tours cruise the New River, past 'Millionaires' Row', and stop at the *Jungle Queen*'s very own jungle island complete with Indian village. The acclaimed and ever popular dinner cruise adds to this a barbecue feast, a vaudeville revue and the assurance of a lively sing-along evening. Adjacent to Bahia-Mar is the Pier 66 Hotel and Marina. Prices here are as high as its famous 17th-floor revolving lounge, but it is well worth the cost of an early evening drink to watch the sunset and view the yachts.

*Continue south on **SR A1A**. Turn left onto Sliphead Road.*

Port Everglades

2 This is the second largest cruise terminal in Florida after Miami, but in terms of luxury tonnage it is number one. If you would like to sample the world of cruising, book a full- or half-day trip on board *SeaEscape* to the Bahamas, or to Nowhere. For no more than the price of a good restaurant meal, the latter lets you experience all the trappings and entertainment you would expect on a luxury cruiser, including its own casino. ('Nowhere' is, of course, simply a sea voyage.) *SeaEscape* also departs from Miami, St Petersburg and Port Canaveral. For lovers of the natural world, however, the stars of the port are the manatees which are attracted to the power company's warm-water creek whenever the temperature of the sea falls below around 68°F (20°C). These gentle giants, members of the sea cow family, can measure up to 15 feet (4.6m) long and weigh up to 1,000 pounds (454kg). Their herbivorous appetite is enormous and makes short work of the whole lettuce heads that visitors throw to them. Exotic reef fish also swim here during winter. The observation area is always open and is one of Florida's favorite freebies (follow the road to the right just past the port entrance).

Rejoin SR A1A for Ocean World.

Ocean World

3 The highlights of this small marine park are the excellent sea lion and dolphin shows. You can demonstrate your appreciation after the show at the popular dolphin petting and feeding tanks. Other areas include shark-feeding, exotic bird shows and playful otters. Round off a good half-day's entertainment by taking Ocean World's own Intracoastal Waterway cruise.

*Continue west on **SR A1A**, cross **US 1** and turn right on SE 3rd Avenue. Drive north to Las Olas Boulevard.*

Board the romantic Jungle Queen *and see the sights at a stately pace cruising along the New River*

Museum of Art

4 The very modern Museum of Art is the setting for two fine collections —the North European CoBrA (Copenhagen–Brussels–Amsterdam) school, and an ethnic range of American Indian, pre-Columbian, West African and Oceanic paintings and sculptures. One block east, the distinctive stepped profile of the city's **Main Library** is a recent striking addition to the modern cityscape, and temporary art exhibitions are often held here. Cross South Andrews Avenue and the New River

BACK TO NATURE

There are two fine state recreation areas (SRAs) immediately to the north and south of the main town beach. The **Hugh Taylor Birch SRA** (north) comprises 180 acres (73 hectares) of undisturbed subtropical splendor with fishing, boating and canoeing facilities, while the larger **John U Lloyd SRA** is particularly noted for its fishing. A nature hike through the park's dunes, coastal hammocks and mangroves is a refreshing contrast to the concrete downtown development. Better still is **Colee Hatchee National Park** (2000 NE 15th Avenue). From boardwalks, visitors can see herons, raccoons and introduced parrots.

FOR CHILDREN

Although older children will probably enjoy boat trips, the duration of many cruises will outweigh the novelty for little ones. Instead, try the **Discovery Center Museum**. Stimulating hands-on experiments in all fields let children bend a ray of light, touch a star, crawl back in time through a cave of bones and fossils, and much more. Adults will also enjoy the experience (due to move in 1992 to form a science museum on SW 2nd Avenue).

SCENIC ROUTES

The most scenic routes in Fort Lauderdale are waterbound, so take a day's rest from driving and climb aboard a riverboat excursion. Another option is to take a water-taxi and ask the captain to take you on one of his very own scenic routes. These small craft can navigate picturesque creeks and inlets that are off-limits to larger craft.

RECOMMENDED WALKS

Close to the Museum of Art off SW 1st Avenue is the recently landscaped palm-lined **New River Walk**. Here you can stroll in the riverside park and enjoy watching the boats sail by from sidewalk cafés. For a more get-away-from-it-all experience, take a ranger-guided walk at one of the state recreation areas.

FOR HISTORY BUFFS

Modern Fort Lauderdale really began in 1901 with Frank Stranahan's remote trading post on the New River. Even 10 years later there were still only 143 white settlers registered in the whole of Broward County's 1,200 square miles (3,108sq km). Stranahan traded peacefully with the Indians, however, and on occasions even allowed them to camp out under his veranda. The best time to learn more about these early days is on a Friday evening at the **Stranahan House** (as the old trading post became), when friendly period-dressed folk from the Historical Society serve drinks and hors d'oeuvres in a delightful turn-of-the-century atmosphere.

Turtle time: wide-ranging imaginative displays enthrall all ages at the Discovery Center Museum

to SW 1st Avenue. The **Broward County Museum of Archaeology** goes far back beyond pioneer days to Ice Age remains, Tequesta Indians and pre-Columbian cultures.

Historical Society Museum/ Himmarshee Village

5 The small Historical Society Museum traces the history of Fort Lauderdale from its pioneering days up to 1945, by means of photographs, costumes and personal artifacts. Put this history into a domestic perspective at the 1907 **King-Cromartie House**, just a few yards away, and admire the ingenuity of antique inventions on display. Adjacent is the historic **New River Inn**, built in 1905 as the city's first hotel. For some years this provided an unlikely home for the first-class **Discovery Center Museum**. The historic district comprises eight square blocks. To see its shops and restaurants, take the drive between the King-Cromartie House and the Discovery Center to SW 3rd Avenue, then head north to Broward Boulevard.

Drive east on Broward Boulevard to SE 3rd Avenue. Turn south onto this road, then left onto Las Olas Boulevard. Continue as far as SE 12th Avenue.

Las Olas Boulevard

6 This exclusive Spanish Colonial shopping street is nationally renowned for its jewelry, haute couture and art and antique galleries, which stretch as far as SE 26th. For a romantic night out on the boulevard, take a horse-and-carriage ride to one of its fine restaurants and do some window shopping by gaslight after dinner. Turn right on SE 26th Avenue to find the **Stranahan House**. Built in 1902, this is the oldest house in Broward County and contains much original furniture.

*Head back towards the ocean and turn left on **SR A1A**. Turn left at Sunrise Boulevard, then left onto North Birch Road.*

Bonnet House

7 Open May to November by reserved tour only, *tel:* (305) 563-5393. This fine Florida-style mansion was built in the 1920s by artist and art collector Frederick Clay Bartlett. The 30 lovely rooms open to the public contain an eclectic and unconventional treasure trove of fine and decorative art. The house sits in 35 beautiful acres (14 hectares), which you can tour in a surrey. A little further north lies another of the city's popular riverboats, the *Paddlewheel Queen*, which cruises the Intracoastal Waterway.

*Head south on **SR A1A** to return to the Voyager station, Bahia-Mar Yacht Center.*

Boca Raton's Mizner Center, named for the man who defined the city's distinctive style

☑ Greater Fort Lauderdale Convention and Visitors Bureau, 500 Broward Boulevard, Suite 104

From Fort Lauderdale head north on Powerline Road (SR 845) for 6 miles (10km) to Atlantic Boulevard.

Pompano Beach

1 The Pompano Harness Track offers the only opportunity in Florida to catch the elegant and exciting sport of harness racing (the harness, or sulky, is little more than a seat suspended between two wheels, and the race is carried out at a trot, not a gallop). Meetings starring the country's top drivers and horses are held from late November through mid-April. Just north off Florida's Turnpike (SR 834) at Sample Road is Butterfly World in Tradewinds Park. A lush indoor tropical rain forest has been created to house thousands of butterflies. Once inside, you will soon become part of this colorful world as its residents flutter around and settle on you (go in the afternoon to avoid school groups). There are also aviaries, boat and bicycle rental, a petting zoo and a small museum.

Take Sample Road east to where it rejoins Powerline Road. Watersports enthusiasts may wish to take a mile (1.5km)-long diversion north to Quiet Waters Park, where—thanks to an overhead automatic cable-pull for water-skiing—the waters are rarely quiet. It is an excellent way to learn the sport and you can watch the more advanced skiers slalom, trick-ski and even ski barefoot! Return to Powerline Road and travel south

Billiards, anyone? Authentic period furnishing in the Flagler Museum

PALM BEACH COUNTY & THE TREASURE COAST

Fort Lauderdale • Pompano Beach
Boca Raton • Delray Beach • Lake Worth
West Palm Beach • Palm Beach • Juno Beach
Jupiter • Hutchinson Island • Jensen Beach
Jonathan Dickinson State Park • Fort Lauderdale

Mention Palm Beach and thoughts turn to polo, Rolls-Royces, peroxide-blond matrons sporting too much gold, and, of course, palm beaches. Here money is everything and nothing. Submerged in 80 feet (24m) of water off Lake Worth lies a 1965 Rolls-Royce, sunk deliberately to give scuba divers something interesting to look at! While such extravagance may not be to everyone's taste, such highly conspicuous consumption nevertheless makes for a memorable visit. You can people-watch and window-shop for free, partake in what you can afford, then go back to the real world with at least a tale or two of high society. Those visitors who 'have to ask the price' will probably want to move on before too long, and the Treasure Coast is a good alternative. People and prices are more down-to-earth here, yet the atmosphere is still calm and often elegant. Commercialism has yet to intrude in a big way along this coast. And of course Palm Beach's sporting action and cultured nightlife are just a short drive away.

A scattering of high-rises fails to overwhelm Palm Beach's elite style

SCENIC ROUTES

The **Indian River Drive (SR 707)**, which runs parallel to the Indian River (actually a lagoon separating the barrier islands from the mainland), is a pretty route cutting through the site of former pineapple plantations. Follow it southwards from Eldred via Walton and Jensen Beach. Further south, the section of **SR 707** from Port Salerno to Jupiter Lighthouse, passing many large banyan trees, is also recommended. If you prefer mansions to trees take **SR A1A** from Hillsboro Beach to Palm Beach.

RECOMMENDED WALKS

The best areas for walking on this tour are the relatively short nature trails at the **Loxahatchee Refuge** and the **Gumbo Limbo Nature Center** at Boca Raton. The latter is an Everglades-style boardwalk trail through dense tropical forest. The gumbo-limbo is a tree of Caribbean origin, nicknamed the 'tourist tree' because in summer its bark turns red and peels.

towards Fort Lauderdale for 3 miles (5km) before turning left onto **Atlantic Drive**. Follow this east to the SR A1A coastal route and turn northwards. Towering above is the 136-foot (41m) skeletal steel tower of the **Hillsboro Inlet lighthouse**, built in 1907 (not open to the public).

Take SR A1A north through Deerfield Beach past its fishing pier.

Boca Raton

2 The name of the city means 'mouth of the rat', and is a reference to the jagged rocks around the coast. This elegant, wealthy community was developed in the 1920s under the guidance of the colorful architect Addison Mizner and is distinguished by its fine Spanish Revival architecture. The highlight of Mizner's surviving work is the extravagant, huge pink **Boca Raton Resort Hotel**. This incorporates his famous 100-room Cloister Inn, built in 1926 as the last word in luxury. The whole complex advertized itself under the headline 'I am the greatest resort in the world'. There is a particularly well-kept beach here and two small museums to explore. Turn left on Park Road (SR 798), cross the bridge, then cross over **US 1** to the **Singing Pines Museum**, with changing exhibits for children. A little further on is the Boca Raton **Museum of the Arts.**

*Continue north on **US 1** for 8 miles (13km).*

Delray Beach

3 Similar in atmosphere to Boca Raton, this attractive resort has been kept deliberately low-key and low-rise. It too boasts a fine beach. Don't miss the beautiful Japanese art, culture and exotic plants at the peaceful **Morikami Museum, Park and Gardens** (west on Atlantic Avenue/SR 806). This unusual attraction is a legacy of an early Japanese farming community in Delray Beach.

*Continue north on **US 1** through Boynton Beach and Lantana, and turn right at Lake Worth Road (SR 802), 11 miles (18km).*

Lake Worth

4 Close to the bridge is the **Lannan Foundation Museum**. This is a dynamic collection of contemporary art, notably paintings, sculptures, glass and ceramics, that claims to be at the forefront of modern fashion. Cross the bridge and you will come to what is, according to locals, the best strip of sand in the whole Palm Beach area.

*Return to **US 1** and head north for 6 miles (10km).*

West Palm Beach

5 This is the mainland part of the famous city, originally built by Henry Flagler as a dormitory town for his railroad workers, and, compared to Palm Beach island, it is still relatively down-to-earth. Today it is a commercial center with a population of 70,000 and is the biggest city in the county. Before you reach downtown, just off **US 1**, is the **South Florida Science Musum**. Children can discover by touch in the Light and

Set in 140 acres (57 hectares) the Morikami Museum presents Japanese folk art. It is a tribute to the area's early Japanese pineapple growers

The landmark Jupiter Lighthouse, guiding ships since 1859, can be seen from waterfront restaurants

Sight Hall, explore the depths in the aquarium, chart the heavens in the observatory, enjoy an evening laser show and more. Adjacent is **Dreher Park and Zoo**, where 29 acres (12 hectares) of lush botanical gardens are home to over 100 species of animals and a delightful walk-through butterfly house.

Return to **US 1** and continue north to the **Norton Gallery of Art**. This is one of America's most highly rated small museums. The core of the collection is major works by French Impressionist and modern masters including such artists as Monet, Gauguin, Matisse, Braque and Pollock. Priceless Chinese jades and bronzes and important sculptures by the likes of Moore, Picasso and Dégas, set in a lovely patio garden, complete this outstanding gallery. You can see more outdoor sculptures and works of art at the **Ann Norton Sculpture Gardens** (afternoons only) half a mile (1km) south.

Continue north and turn right onto Royal Palm Way, 2 miles (3km).

Palm Beach

6 The stately colonnade of Royal Palm Way is a fitting processional route into one of the world's most monied communities. Turn left on Cocoanut Row to see the home of Henry Morrison Flagler, who created Palm Beach by bringing his railroad to southern Florida. **Whitehall** was the 73-room mansion that Flagler gave to his third wife as a wedding present in 1901, and since 1959 it has functioned as a museum. Its palatial great halls, music room, billiards room, library, dining rooms and bedrooms are decorated in historic European styles and give an idea of the lifestyle enjoyed in that pioneering era by Flagler and such illustrious guests as the Vanderbilts, Woodrow Wilson, John Jacob Astor and William Rockefeller. This is also the perfect place to learn more about the Florida East Coast Railroad, and you can even board Flagler's personal railroad car, 'Rambler'.

Continue on Cocoanut Row to Royal Poinciana Plaza. Among the exclusive shops here—a foretaste of Worth Avenue—is the **Hibel Museum of Art**. The only public non-profit gallery in the country dedicated to a living woman artist, it features the work of Edna Hibel, famous for her humanitarian efforts. Continue north, past the elegant **Palm Beach Biltmore** (now condominiums), built in 1927 at a cost of $7 million. The road becomes Lake Way, and parallel to it the **Palm Beach Bicycle Trail** runs for almost 5 miles (8km). The mansions along this route are some of the finest and most expensive in the county, hence the trail is known as 'the world's most beautiful cycle path'. Continue to the end of the island and glance across to **Peanut Island**. Here is the site of the Kennedys' atomic bomb shelter, built during the Cuban missile crisis.

Return south on Ocean Boulevard. Just past Royal Poinciana Way — Palm Beach's other regal entrance route — is the beautiful church of **Bethesda-by-the-Sea**, built in 1927. Next is **The Breakers**, the legendary hotel built by Flagler in Italian Renaissance style in 1926 and still one of the benchmarks of high society today. On Sundays non-residents can sample The Breakers' lifestyle at the Beach Club Champagne Brunch, said to be the biggest in the state. Continue to the eastern end of Worth Avenue. This is one of the world's great shopping streets, where Cartier, Hermes, Chanel, Gucci and Saks Fifth Avenue are just everyday names among the 250 or so glittering stores on and around the avenue. However, it is not just the names and prices that make Worth Avenue great — it is the atmosphere created by the manicured palms, the beautiful Addison Mizner Spanish-style architecture and the quaint, not to mention outrageously expensive, shops and cafés tucked away in tiny alleyways.

Cross back to the mainland by Royal Palm Way, turn right onto **US 1** *and continue north for 8 miles (13km).*

Juno Beach

7 Juno Beach, Jupiter and Jensen Beach are all nesting grounds for sea turtles, and at the **Loggerhead Park Marine Life Center** in Juno Beach you can learn more about their habits. The center also features aquariums and various exhibits on local coastal life.

Take **US 1** *north, turning left to Jupiter.*

Jupiter

8 The **Jupiter Theatre**, on SR A1A, was donated to the community by its most famous son, actor Burt Reynolds. Opened in 1979, it regularly plays host to stars of Broadway and Hollywood. Head east to US 1, turn right onto Jupiter Island and visit the small but pleasant **Loxahatchee Historical Society Museum**. You can't miss the bright red **Jupiter Lighthouse**, looming 105 feet (32m) above you. Completed in 1859, it is the county's oldest structure (open Sunday afternoons). Take SR 707 north to **Blowing Rocks Preserve**, a beachfront nature reserve of some 73 acres (30 hectares). At high tide, particularly during storms, the breaking waves are forced up through fissures and holes in the limestone rocks and 'blow' upwards creating dramatic plumes.

Continue north on **SR 707** *through Jupiter Island and rejoin the mainland. Continue north to Stuart and turn right onto Hutchinson Island, 24 miles (39km).*

Hutchinson Island

9 At the southern end of the island lies the (Gilbert's Bar) **House of Refuge Museum** (open afternoons). The House of Refuge was built in 1875 to function as a coastguard station, including a lookout tower and

dormitory accommodation for up to 24 shipwreck survivors. It is the only one of its kind left in Florida. The dormitory is closed to the public, but you can see the prettily restored rooms where the keeper and his wife lived. The old boathouse is now the front desk area, full of salty nautical memorabilia, and there is a small aquarium below. The rocky coves and sandy beach make for a picturesque setting and good snorkeling, while just south of here is **Bathtub Beach**, a favorite spot for families. A mile (1.5km) to the north of the House of Refuge is the eclectic and colorful **Elliott Museum** (afternoons only). This large collection comprises an 'Americana Corridor' of antique shopfronts, a 'Gracious Living Wing' featuring period parlors from all over the world, and a '1914 Garage' with a very fine collection of vintage automobiles. Follow the road north to the **St Lucie County Historical Museum**. Here you can see artifacts relating to Spanish shipwrecks and Seminole Indians, and a guide will take you around the adjacent 1907 **Gardner House**.

Cross over to the mainland and turn left, heading south on **US 1**. *Pass through Fort Pierce and follow* **SR 707** *south, 38 miles (61km).*

Jensen Beach

10 Each year at this 'Sea Turtle Capital of the World' some 6,000 of the creatures come to Jensen and surrounding beaches to lay their eggs. A 'turtle watch' is conducted by the **Environmental Studies Center** on Jensen Beach each June and July. If you would like to see loggerhead and perhaps leatherback turtles nesting on the beach at this time, you can join a group by reservation; phone (407) 334-3444.

Turn right to rejoin **US 1** *and follow this south for 16 miles (26km).*

Jonathan Dickinson State Park

11 At over 10,000 acres (4,047 hectares) this is one of south Florida's largest parks. The wild and scenic Loxahatchee River runs through the park, whose abundant wildlife, particularly birds, flourishes in a diversity of ecosystems. Ranger-guided tours and trips aboard the 30-seater *Loxahatchee Queen* are run year-round. Canoes and rowboats are also available for rent.

Continue south on **US 1** *for 68 miles (110km) to return to Fort Lauderdale.*

Fort Lauderdale–Pompano Beach **6 (10)**
Pompano Beach–Boca Raton **18 (29)**
Boca Raton–Delray Beach **8 (13)**
Delray Beach–Lake Worth **11 (18)**
Lake Worth–West Palm Beach **6 (10)**
West Palm Beach–Palm Beach **2 (3)**
Palm Beach–Juno Beach **8 (13)**
Juno Beach–Jupiter **6 (10)**
Jupiter–Hutchinson Island **24 (39)**
Hutchinson Island–Jensen Beach **38 (61)**
Jensen Beach–Jonathan Dickinson State Park **16 (26)**
Jonathan Dickinson State Park–Fort Lauderdale **68 (110)**

SPECIAL TO . . .

6 *Palm Beach* Palm Beach is famous the world over for polo and is the only place in Florida where the sport is played professionally. The most famous club is the **Palm Beach Polo and Country Club** at West Palm Beach, where Prince Charles plays. There are two other clubs open to the public, the **Gulfstream Polo Grounds** at Lake Worth and the **Royal Palm Beach** at Boca Raton. You can mix with the 'beautiful people' every Sunday from December through April.

FOR HISTORY BUFFS

6 *Palm Beach* **The Breakers**, probably the most famous hotel in Florida, encapsulates the pioneering spirit of the early days on the East Coast. A guided tour of the hotel is conducted every Wednesday. Tales of Flagler's legendary East Coast Railroad are, of course, de rigueur, but you will also hear about the hotel's use during Prohibition and how it served briefly as a hostel during World War II.

FOR CHILDREN

6 *Palm Beach* **Lion Country Safari**, 15 miles (24km) west of Palm Beach on Southern Boulevard/SR 80, is the only self-drive safari park in Florida. Here over a thousand animals roam freely over hundreds of acres of natural wildlife preserve. Close encounters with lions, elephants, rhinos, zebras, giraffes, ostriches and inquisitive monkeys are all part of the excitement. An amusement park with rides, games, a petting zoo and a river cruise completes a good half-day's entertainment.

BACK TO NATURE

8 *Jupiter* The **Loxahatchee National Wildlife Refuge** comprises over 221 square miles (572sq km) of unspoiled Everglades. You can see this beautiful wilderness from an airboat or you can rent your own motorboat or canoe. There are two nature trails, one through a cypress swamp (look out for barrel owls), the other across a marsh to an observation tower. Bird-watchers should look out for the rare snail kite, as well as rails, limpkins and herons, while anglers can enjoy some of the finest big bass fishing in the country. To get there take Atlantic Avenue **(SR 806)** west from Delray Beach.

CENTRAL GULF COAST

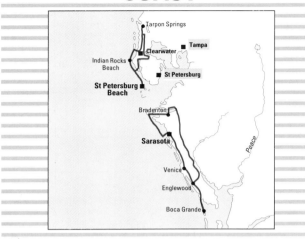

Tour 8
The tour starts with the coastal vacation area known as the Pinellas. This is fast becoming the most popular choice for the second week of suntanning (after the obligatory week at Walt Disney World) in the typical family vacation in Florida. Clearwater and St Petersburg Beach are the best-equipped resorts, offering excellent beaches and plenty to do for all ages, both day and night. To the north the fascinating Greek enclave of Tarpon Springs is a unique sponge-fishing community.

City Tour 5
Most Pinellas sun worshippers will take a day or two off the beach to explore the town of St Petersburg, if only to shop the new malls and The Pier. The town is quiet, pleasant and almost belies its two outstanding art galleries. The Salvador Dali Collection could well turn out to be the most unexpected highlight of a whole fortnight in Florida.

Idyllic white sands and blue skies embrace Clearwater Beach

This is Florida's fastest-growing tourist region, and comparisons with the rival traditional destinations of Miami and the Gold Coast are inevitable. Around a century ago both coasts were being developed apace by the two great railroad pioneers of the day, Henry Morrison Flagler and Henry Bradley Plant. As Flagler built his splendid Spanish-Mediterranean piles from St Augustine to Palm Beach, so Plant saw the potential on the west coast, brought his tracks south from Virginia, and created the magnificent Moroccan-style Tampa Bay Hotel.

In 1891 Plant sent an invitation to his rival to attend the opening of his new hotel in Tampa. Flagler's reply simply read 'Where's Tampa?' As far as the development of Florida went, Flagler again had the last word, for while Plant's tracks went no further south, Flagler's stretched the entire length of the Atlantic Coast.

It was not until the development of Busch Gardens in the last two decades that tourists have stopped asking, 'Where's Tampa?' While it is still true that, Busch Gardens aside, the city of Tampa has much less to offer the visitor than does Miami, the central west coast resorts, which stretch from Clearwater to Sarasota, do have a number of advantages over their long-established east-coast counterparts.

Nature has endowed this coast with a near-perfect climate, beaches that are better, a sea that is warmer and sunsets that are more glorious. Man-made attractions are almost as numerous as those on the east, while man-made intrusions (most notably, ugly canyons of condominiums) are far less common. Best of all for families, prices are lower here.

The atmosphere is more relaxed and less fashion-conscious. There are few *Miami Vice*-style cigar boats to admire, but then again there are few of the problems associated with that city and its type of fast lifestyle. Neither is the Gulf Coast all pensioners on park benches and children toting sand buckets. St Pete and Clearwater each have a bustling nightlife, while Sarasota is as stylish and attractive an all-round resort as you will find anywhere in the state. In summary, the Central Gulf Coast contains a little of everything required for a good vacation and, for most families, a perfect package.

City Tour 6

Tampa is quite a contrast to St Petersburg, with its skyscrapers, central business district, diverse industries and ethnic influences giving it the feel of a big city. As a magnet for tourism Tampa has long been in the shadow of Busch Gardens, and it is only recently, with the revitalization of Ybor City and the developments on Harbour Island, that it is beginning to woo tourists.

Tour 9

Across the magnificent Sunshine Skyway bridge, it would seem that the only factor preventing Sarasota breaking into the big league of tourism is its lack of children's attractions. Aside from this it has wonderful beaches, the priceless Ringling complex, sophisticated shopping and dining and a cultural program that is second to none. For those who do not have to worry about amusing children, it is a very attractive proposition.

Stomach-churning terror aboard the 'Python', Busch Gardens

2 days – 78 miles (125km)

THE PINELLAS SUNCOAST

St Petersburg Beach • Treasure Island
Madeira Beach/Indian Rocks Beach
Clearwater Beach • Dunedin • Tarpon Springs
Boatyard Village/Aviation Museum
Heritage Park and Museum • St Petersburg Beach

At a meeting in 1885 the American Medical Association pronounced that the Pinellas area (the name is Spanish for pines) boasted the ideal climate and location for a 'world health city'. It is a fact that few places enjoy as much sun as the Pinellas (on average 361 days per year), and *The Guinness Book of Records* confirms it as the sunniest place on earth, having recorded 768 consecutive days between February 1967 and March 1969. Given that this area also has 28 miles (45km) of wide, clean, safe, white sand beaches, it is hardly surprising that it is the most popular vacation destination on the west coast of Florida, particularly for families.

Bustling St Petersburg Beach is lined with restaurants, beach bars and well-kept mid-rise hotels. Unmissable among these is the candy-pink *Don CeSar*, built in 1927 in a whimsical Moorish-Mediterranean style that resembles a gigantic sandcastle. Its guest book reads like a *Who's Who* (F Scott Fitzgerald and Babe Ruth stayed at the Don in its heyday). The *Silas Dent Bayside Market*, featuring shopping, a food court, a wax museum and a fun house, is the newest attraction at St Pete Beach.

SPECIAL TO . . .

There is no single outstanding festival in the Pinellas calender, but the following are all recommended:
April—**Fun 'n' Sun** in Clearwater, a carnival with a 40-year-old tradition;
June—**Sandcastle Contest** on St Pete Beach, to witness some amazing sand creations; first week in July—**Pirate Days and Invasion** at Treasure Island; last weekend in October—**John's Pass Seafood Festival**, including music, arts and crafts.

🛈 St Petersburg Beach Chamber of Commerce, 6990 Gulf Boulevard

Head north on Gulf Boulevard for 4 miles (6km).

Treasure Island/John's Pass Village

1 This area of beach—named for its long association with pirates—is slightly quieter than St Pete Beach and is about half its size, with older low-rise accommodation. Just across the bridge to Madeira Beach is John's Pass Village and Boardwalk. This charmingly restored fishermen's village comprises some 60 ramshackle-looking tin-roofed wooden structures housing restaurants,

Natural sponges, gathered from deep waters, are trimmed into shape before going on sale

shops, and galleries, linked by a boardwalk perched high above the water. Fishing is both an important industry and a tourist attraction here, and boats can be chartered. If you prefer a pleasure cruise, the *Europa Sun* will take you out by day or night.

🛈 Treasure Island Chamber of Commerce, 152 108th Avenue

Continue on Gulf Boulevard for 3 miles (5km).

Madeira Beach/Indian Rocks Beach

2 The name Madeira is derived from *madera*, referring like *pinellas* to pine woods. This long coastal stretch of some 7 miles (11km) is the least interesting of the Holiday Isles, with large characterless hotels and high-rise condominiums. Redington Pier, stretching over 1,000 feet (305m) into the Gulf, makes a welcome punctuation mark and is very popular with fishing folk. The **Suncoast Seabird Sanctuary** is certainly worth a visit. This is the largest wild bird hospital in the country, rehabilitating and releasing some 15 to 20 birds per day. Those that cannot survive on their own become residents; these can number up to 500, of which around a third are usually pelicans. Ask the staff what time the day's 'outpatients' are to be discharged and watch them return to the wild. At Indian Rocks Beach is **Hamlin's Landing**, a large, rambling Victorian shopping and dining complex on the Intracoastal Waterway. This is the home of the *Starlight Princess*, a triple-deck paddlewheel cruiser offering excursions along the inland waters.

🛈 The Gulf Beaches Chamber of Commerce, 501 150th Avenue

Continue north and cross the Clearwater Pass causeway.

Clearwater Beach

3 Clearwater is the liveliest of the Pinellas beaches, popular with young couples and teenagers, and is stocked with all the usual beachside facilities for their enjoyment. A number of cruises depart from Clearwater Beach Marina, and recommended among these is **Captain Memo's Pirate Cruise**. Decorated and themed in buccaneer fashion the *Sea Hogge* cruises the scenic Intracoastal Waterway and sails out into the Gulf —though you don't actually get to raid anywhere and all the crew members are female!

Turn east toward the mainland on the Garden Memorial Causeway (**SR 60**), turn left at Island Way, then left onto Windward Passage and continue for two blocks to the **Clearwater Marine Science Center and Aquarium**. This coastal research station is dedicated to the rescue and rehabilitation of stranded sea mammals and turtles. Among other

The Marina at Clearwater, the place to catch a sightseeing cruise or charter a fishing boat

RECOMMENDED WALKS

The Holiday Isles beachfront communities are not suitable for walking, either in terms of layout or for points of interest. However, you can take an interesting self-guided tour of **Tarpon Springs** by picking up a leaflet from the town's cultural center. To get away from it all you can walk the full 4 miles (6km) around **Caladesi Island** or take any one of the several nature trails at **Moccasin Lake Park** or **Fort De Soto Park.**

BACK TO NATURE

4 *Dunedin* **Caladesi Island State Park** is one of Florida's few undeveloped barrier islands. On the harbor side a mangrove swamp provides refuge for wading and shore birds, while the interior is virgin pine and oak hammocks. A 3-mile (5km) self-guided nature trail leads through here to an observation tower. Snowy egrets, herons, armadillos and 'gators are often spotted.

residents you can meet Sunset Sam and Thunder, two bottle-nosed dolphins, and Big Mo, a 400-pound (180kg) loggerhead turtle. Return to the Memorial Causeway and continue east to US 19(Alt). If you would like to see one of Florida's grandest hotels, make a diversion by turning right onto Fort Harrison Avenue **US 19(Alt)**, drive south 1 mile (1.5km) and turn right onto Belleview Boulevard. The **Belleview Biltmore**, creation of Henry B Plant (see Tampa), opened its ornate doors in 1887. It is claimed to be the world's largest lived-in wooden structure (the roof covers 2½ acres/1 hectare).

The sumptuous interior features Tiffany glass and crystal chandeliers and the guest list once included the Duke of Windsor. Recently renovated by its Japanese owners, it is now known as the Belleview Midois.

ⓘ Welcome Center, 40 Causeway Boulevard

Turn right and continue north for 5 miles (8km) to the junction with Main Street **(SR 580)**.

Dunedin

4 The Gaelic accent to this small old-fashioned town comes from its Scottish founders. The bagpipes can still be heard on the first Sunday of each month, and every March/April a festival of **Highland Games** is staged. Dunedin is also famous locally for its antique shops and its romantically named offshore islands, Honeymoon and Caladesi (the latter meaning 'beautiful bayou'). You can drive to **Honeymoon Island** but for **Caladesi Island** you will have to catch the passenger ferry as no cars are allowed.

ⓘ Chamber of Commerce, 434 Main Street

Continue north for 8 miles (13km) to Tarpon Springs.

Named for the patron saint of sailors, like the local church, this vessel takes tourists around Tarpon Springs' fine sponge beds

Tarpon Springs

5 'America's Sponge Capital' really took off around 1905 with the discovery of high-quality sponge beds in the Gulf of Mexico quite close by. Expert Greek sponge-fishermen and divers were recruited from Key West and from Greece itself, and by the 1930s Tarpon Springs had become the biggest sponge port in the world. A disastrous blight wiped out most of the beds in the 1940s, but in recent years they have recovered. Despite these vagaries the long-established close-knit Greek community still flourishes, and you can dive into any one of several *tavernas* for authentic Greek cuisine, complete with *bouzouki* music and sweet, sticky *baklava* pastries. Take a boat tour, complete with a Jules Verne-style sponge-diver equipped with canvas suit, spherical helmet and leaded boots. Back at the dock, **Spongeorama** is a free exhibit on the history of sponge fishing in the area; if you want to see more, there is another small **museum** in the old **Sponge Exchange** (now a shopping mall) by the dock. Adjacent to this is the **Coral Sea Aquarium**, where huge open-air tanks teem with indigenous sea creatures and exotic species from the Pacific Ocean. On your way out of town, stop on the main road to admire the marbled

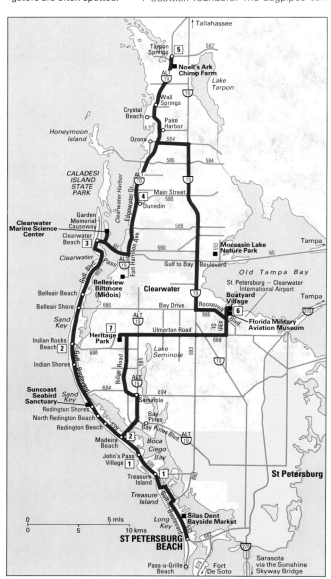

Echoes of Jules Verne: turn-of-the-century improvements in deep-sea diving equipment determined the future character of Tarpon Springs

interior of the Greek Orthodox **Church of St Nicholas** built in 1943 as a replica of the Byzantine church of Haghia Sophia in Istanbul.

Just outside town is **Noell's Ark Chimp Farm**. The displays at this well-meaning refuge for rejected primates and other animals are unfortunately not of a high standard.

ⓘ Cultural Center, Old City Hall, South Pinellas Avenue, **US 19**(Alt); Chamber of Commerce, 210 South Pinellas Avenue, **US 19**(Alt)

*South of Tarpon Springs turn left onto **SR 584** and turn right to join **US 19** southbound. Continue for around 13 miles (21km) and turn left onto Roosevelt Boulevard (**SR 686**). Turn left on 49th Street, then take the first right.*

Boatyard Village

6 The **aviation museum** houses a collection of a dozen fighting and transport aircraft plus military vehicles and weapon systems (many of these are outdoors so you can see them through the fence for free). The adjacent **94th Aero Squadron restaurant** continues the theme, featuring memorabilia from World War I. Boatyard Village, which looks onto Tampa Bay, is an amazing re-creation of a turn-of-the-century New England fishing village, built of aged wood and tin from around the country. Within the rustic alleyways and rambling boardwalks you will find some fine shops, atmospheric restaurants and a theater.

*Return to 49th Street and head south. Turn right on Ulmerton Road (**SR 688**) and continue for 5 miles (8km). Two blocks west of Missouri Boulevard/**US 19 (Alt)** turn left onto 125th Street.*

Heritage Park and Museum

7 Fourteen of the county's oldest structures have been brought to this 21-acre (8-hectare) leafy pine and palm park to give you an idea of what an early settlement may have looked like in its entirety. Visit the small **museum** to learn about Pinellas County history, then join a period-dressed guide who will show you around the properties. These include a railroad station, a store, a church and the oldest surviving log house in Pinellas County. Basic pioneer skills such as spinning and weaving are often demonstrated.

*Return one block east to Ridge Road, turn right and head south for 5 miles (8km) to Madeira Causeway/Bay Pines Boulevard, **US 19**(Alt). Turning right will take you back to the coast road and St Petersburg Beach; turning left will take you into the town of St Petersburg.*

St Petersburg Beach–Treasure Island **4 (6)**
Treasure Island–Madeira Beach **3 (5)**
Madeira Beach–Clearwater Beach **14 (23)**
Clearwater Beach–Dunedin **5 (8)**
Dunedin–Tarpon Springs **8 (13)**
Tarpon Springs–Boatyard Village **20 (32)**
Boatyard Village–Heritage Park **9 (14)**
Heritage Park–St Petersburg Beach **15 (24)**

FOR HISTORY BUFFS

Fort De Soto, named after the Spanish discoverer of this coast, was built in 1898 to protect the Gulf shipping lanes during the Spanish–American War. Its intervention was never required, however, and you can see its unused 12-inch (305mm) mortars.

SCENIC ROUTES

The Sunshine Skyway is a suspension bridge finished in 1987 at a cost of $244 million. It measures 4.1 miles (6.6km) long and is suspended 183 feet (56m) above the water. The old bridge collapsed in 1980 with the loss of 30 lives after being rammed by a boat. It is currently being converted into Florida's longest fishing pier. Take the Sunshine Skyway for an excursion to **Sarasota**; returning in the evening you can admire the illuminated cables high above you.

FOR CHILDREN

St Petersburg The all-new **Silas's Funhouse and Wax Museum** at St Pete Beach uses holograms and special effects to create a total family attraction.

3 *Clearwater Beach* **Moccasin Lake Nature Park** on Park Trail Lane is a wildlife preserve with several small animal exhibits, an aviary and an interpretive center.

AROUND ST PETERSBURG

**Sunken Gardens • Museum of Fine Arts
St Petersburg Historical Museum/The Pier
Port of St Petersburg • Dali Museum
Great Explorations • Central Avenue
Sunken Gardens**

St Petersburg takes its name from the hometown of Peter Demens, a Russian émigré who built the Orange Belt Railroad into the town in 1888 and stayed to become a driving force in its development. During those early days the idyllic climate of St Pete (as the city is fondly known) attracted a large number of retirees. The elderly are still here, but St Pete also attracts young families and these days is in buoyant mood with all the facilities one would expect of a thrusting modern resort town. Major new sports, entertainment and retail complexes have all been completed within the last three years. The city is not short on culture either, and the decision in 1982 to site the *Dali Museum*—the world's largest collection of the king of the surrealists—was another coup for St Pete. Nevertheless, St Petersburg remains generally quiet, always refined. Ironically, a trip here can make a welcome break from the hustle and bustle of the beach.

ℹ Chamber of Commerce, 100 2nd Avenue North

Start your tour at Sunken Gardens, driving due east from the beaches via 22nd Avenue North as far as 4th Street North, then south to 18th Avenue North.

Sunken Gardens

1 These 5 acres (2 hectares) of luxurious tropical gardens are landscaped around a sinkhole and shallow

The Salvador Dali Museum: collected works date from 1914 and include sculpture and Impressionism

lake, hence the name. Some 50,000 flowers (around 5,000 species) are planted here annually, and there are over 500 exotic birds and animals to admire. The walk-through aviary, is a highlight of this tranquil spot. On site is also a **biblical wax museum**.

Drive south on 4th Street North to 2nd Avenue North and turn left. Drop by the Chamber of Commerce (corner of 1st Street), and continue to Bayshore Drive and park your car.

Museum of Fine Arts

2 This outstanding collection is housed in a handsome Palladian/Mediterranean-style building. Among the museum's most important holdings are outstanding European, pre-Columbian, ancient and Far Eastern art, contemporary photographs and complete Jacobean and Georgian rooms. The gallery of French Impressionism and the brilliantly displayed Steuben crystal are perennial favorites, while the traveling exhibits are frequently of international caliber. Take a free guided tour to get the most from your visit.

Walk along 2nd Avenue towards The Pier, noting 'Comfort Station Number 1' built in 1927.

St Petersburg Historical Museum/The Pier

3 Local and state history is covered in this tiny museum, which supplements its small permanent collection (including Egyptian mummies) with lively changing exhibits. Complimentary trolley cars shuttle to and from **The Pier**, a complex of specialty shops, restaurants and an aquarium housed in a five-story inverted pyramid. There are fine views from the observation platform.

Drive back along 2nd Avenue North, turn left on 1st Street, past Al Lang Field (spring training camp of the St Louis Cardinals) and the multipurpose Bayfront Center. Follow the road around to the left.

Port of St Petersburg

4 This is one of four Florida docking points for SeaEscape, the firm that pioneered 'the cruise to Nowhere'. A circular cruise takes you out beyond the state boundary so that you can enjoy a wager in the casino and generally experience life aboard a major cruise liner, but for a fraction of the usual price. *Ocean Spirit* will take you to the western Caribbean for seven nights to Cozumel, Belize and the Bay Islands.

Return to and turn north onto 1st Street, take the second left (not to the USF campus) and turn left on 3rd Street.

Dali Museum

5 Whatever your preconceptions may be of the work of this flawed genius, do not miss a visit to this

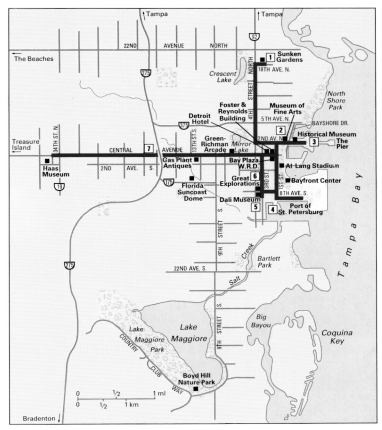

intriguing collection. Free guided tours will take you through Dali's earliest (quite conventional) works to the brilliant precision *trompe l'oeil* and double-image techniques of his surrealist period. You will also learn the meaning of his unforgettable 'soft watches' and lots more about his bizarre imagery. There is a total of 93 oils, over 100 watercolors and hundreds more works, displayed on a rotating basis. Most people's favorites are his 'masterworks', the five works that occupied him for a year or more and measure at least 5 feet (1.5m) in any one direction.

Turn left outside the museum and walk across the street.

Great Explorations

6 All ages can explore this hands-on facility that focuses on the arts, science and personal health. **Phenomenal Arts** creates high-tech artistry by touch or audio-activation, the **Touch Tunnel** is a pitch-black maze for children to negotiate, and the **Body Shop** measures your fitness level. Avoid weekday mornings when school field trips arrive.

Return to your car, drive back north along 3rd Street for seven blocks and turn left.

Central Avenue

7 St Petersburg's main street is an interesting mixture of renovated 1920s buildings and modern developments. Heading west you will pass the 1909 **Foster and Reynolds Building** (1st Street South) and opposite is the brand-new **Bay Plaza** waterfront retail district. The **Detroit Hotel** (now a youth hostel) was St Pete's very first hotel back in 1888.

Five blocks west is the **Green-Richman Arcade**, built in 1923 in the popular Mediterranean Revival style. Five blocks further along, **Gas Plant Antiques** boasts the biggest collection of antiques and collectibles on the west coast of Florida. From

The distinctive Pier, a well-known landmark on Florida's west coast

here you can see the landmark $110 million **Florida Suncoast Dome**. This state-of-the-art sports and entertainment arena is the only enclosed stadium in Florida, and if no event is in progress you are welcome to look inside.

Central Avenue leads directly west to Treasure Island. SR 693, off Central Avenue, leads to St Petersburg Beach.

TAMPA

Downtown Business District • University of Tampa
Harbour Island • Ybor City • Ybor Square
Seventh Avenue • Lowry Park Zoo
Busch Gardens • Museum of Science and Industry
Downtown Business District

Tampa is not only the regional business center, it boasts the country's seventh largest port, *US Operations Command HQ* at MacDill Air Force Base, nearby phosphate mining, beer flowing from Anheuser-Busch and cigars rolled by the million. The last two products are central to Tampa's tourists, even if they are nonsmoking teetotalers. *Busch Gardens*, which started life as a modest brewery hospitality center in 1959, is now the biggest attraction on Florida's west coast. By contrast, the Cuban enclave of *Ybor City* (pronounced Ee-bor) was the cigar capital of the world from 1886 until the 1930s, when the invention of an efficient cigar-rolling machine put thousands of skilled workers out of a job. It is now a preserved historic district and Tampa's second biggest visitor attraction.

Skyscrapers, a sign of Tampa's commercial growth, are never far from more leisurely pursuits

ⓘ Tampa/Hillsborough Convention and Visitors Association (THCVA), Ground Floor, First Florida Tower

*Downtown is easily accessible from **I-275** (exit 25, Ashley Drive) or the Crosstown Expressway (Florida Avenue exit). Park at Old Fort Brooke Garage on Whiting Street, which runs east–west between Ashley Drive and Florida Avenue. Walk west two blocks to Ashley Drive and then north for three blocks.*

Downtown Business District

1 Much of the business and financial hub of the city has been built during the last 20 years. The tallest building in the city is the 42-story **Barnett Bank**, and opposite is the First Florida Tower (home to the local convention and visitors association). The rotund landmark on the Hillsborough River is the **NCNB Bank**. Walk through its plaza to the acclaimed **Tampa Museum of Art**. This holds one of the finest collections of Roman and Greek antiquities in the US, plus sculptures, contemporary American photographs, expressionist works and other fine arts exhibits.

Return to the NCNB Bank and cross the bridge (Kennedy Boulevard).

University of Tampa/Henry B Plant Museum

2 Set in the beautifully landscaped gardens of the university is an amazing Moorish structure with 13 'onion-domed' silver minarets, each crowned with a crescent moon. This was originally the **Tampa Bay Hotel**, built in the style of the Alhambra Palace by Henry B Plant in 1890, at a staggering cost of $2 million. Touring the world in search of furniture and art treasures for the hotel, Plant spent another $1 million. The hotel

A former bakery is now a museum devoted to the cigar industry. Cigars are still hand-rolled locally

SCENIC ROUTES

The 6-mile (10km) sidewalk of Bayshore Boulevard, on the other side of the Hillsborough River from downtown Tampa, is said to be the world's longest continuous walkway. You can walk it, but a slow drive with its fine views of Hillsborough Bay is much more preferable. At the north end of the boulevard, you can cross to elegant Davis Island, a residential neighborhood built on three man-made islands in the 1920s.

shut down in 1929, and the University of Tampa acquired the building in 1933. A **museum** set up in one wing exhibits Plant's sumptuous collection, and a guided tour will take you around the rest of the hotel; reservations *tel:* (813) 253-6220.

Return to Old Fort Brooke Garage, go to the third floor and board the Peoplemover, a continuous-service monorail that links downtown to Harbour Island via an elevated track.

Harbour Island

3 Your monorail journey high above the Garrison Channel takes some 90 seconds. Harbour Island is Tampa's version of Miami's Bayside Marketplace or Jacksonville's Landing: a waterside complex of specialty shopping, restaurants, a food court, nightclubs plus an aquarium. As yet it lacks the panache of the aforementioned and the water views are not so good, but it is still worth a visit. You can take to the water on a paddleboat or board an authentic 70-year-old Venetian gondola for a romantic cruise, complete with Italian opera music.

Return to your car, drive east on Whiting Street, turn right on Morgan Street and left on East Platt Street which runs into 13th Street. Follow this north for approximately 4 miles (6km) to the junction with 9th Avenue. Turn right onto 9th Avenue and drive east to 18th Street.

Ybor City

4 Start your tour of this historic district at the **Ybor City State Museum**, housed in the 1923 Ferlita Bakery (closed Sunday). This will give you a thorough introduction to the history of this colorful, predominantly Cuban community and its cigar-making industry. Adjacent are six renovated turn-of-the-century cigar workers' houses. One of these is open as a small **museum**, another houses the Ybor City Chamber of Commerce, which provides tourist information. Drive along the avenue for four blocks and turn left onto 14th Street. At the corner with 9th Avenue stop to admire the beautiful Spanish-American architecture of the former El Pasaje Hotel (now the **Café Creole**), built in 1896. Park at any of the three lots around the adjacent block which features Ybor Square.

Ybor Square

5 The three enormous three-story brick buildings here are the warehouse, the factory and the stemmery (where leaves and stems were separated) that once employed some 4,000 cigar workers. These atmospheric, sturdy turn-of-the-century buildings have been converted into a dining and shopping complex. Of special note among the many fine specialty and antique stores are the **Tampa Rico Cigar Company** ('Thank You For Smoking'), which preserves the tradition of hand-rolling, and the **Red Horse,** a shop with a nostalgic and very comprehensive collection of old Florida postcards.

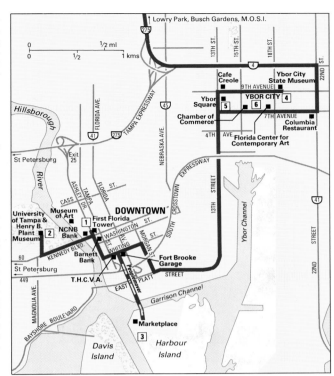

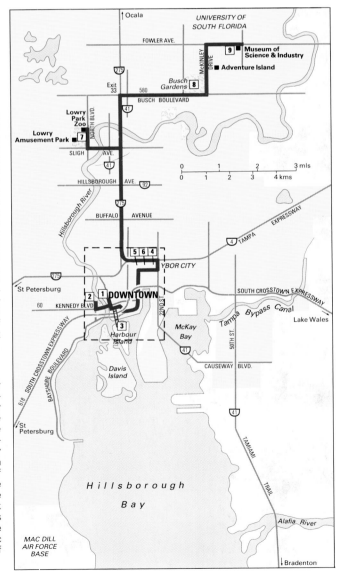

SPECIAL TO . . .

In late January/early February the clock is turned back to buccaneering days for the **Gasparilla Pirate Invasion**. A sort of Mardi Gras with peg-legs and parrots, it features an 'attack' by the triple-masted galleon *José Gaspar* and ensuing parades, concerts, fiestas and all manner of events.

FOR CHILDREN

7 *Lowry Park Zoo* Kids love Busch Gardens and Adventure Island. However, if you have very young children in tow and don't want to spend the whole day and/or a lot of money, then Lowry Park Zoo is a good alternative. The animals here are superbly presented, and the adjacent **Children's Museum** is ideal for toddlers.

Tiger, tiger, burning bright: a stunning white tiger relaxes in a natural setting at Busch Gardens

Drive one block south to 7th Avenue and turn left.

Seventh Avenue

6 As the main street of Ybor City, 7th Avenue contains several historic buildings, most notably the 1917 **Ritz Theater** at 15th Street and the 1894 **Italian Club** at 18th Street. Opposite the latter is the **Florida Center for Contemporary Art**, Tampa's premier alternative visual arts showcase. Four blocks down is one of the oldest and most famous restaurants in Florida, **The Columbia**, established in 1905. It is both an aesthetic and gastronomic delight, with ornate tile-work inside and out, superb Spanish/Cuban food and famous flamenco dancing.

*Head east on 7th Avenue to 22nd Street. Head north and turn left onto **I-4**, west. Bear right onto **I-275** north. Exit at Sligh Avenue, head west and turn right onto North Boulevard.*

Lowry Park Zoo

7 Recently renovated and lushly landscaped, this fine zoo displays its residents in as natural settings as possible. The highlights are a huge free-flight aviary with over 65 sub-tropical species of birds, Primate World, Sumatran tigers and a new Manatee Aquatic Center. Adjacent to the zoo is **Lowry Amusement Park**, with castles, characters from Mother Goose and other stories, amusement rides, a playground, miniature railroad and small zoo.

*Return east to join **I-275**. Head north for 2 miles (3km), turn off at exit 33 (Busch Boulevard/**SR 580**) and continue for 2 miles (3km) to McKinley Drive (40th Street).*

Busch Gardens

8 After Walt Disney World, Busch Gardens is the most visited theme park in Florida and merits a whole day's visit. The theme is turn-of-the-century Africa—a motif stretched somewhat to include such entertainment as an ice show, a Bavarian beer keller with sing-along with 'Sounds of the Sixties'—with a magnificent collection of over 3,300 animals. Don't miss the white tigers, the koalas, the elephants, the bird and dolphin shows and the animal nursery. You can see the gardens on foot, by train or by monorail. The highly acclaimed roller coasters include the 360-degree looping Python, and there is white-water rafting at the Congo River Rapids and the Tanganyika Tidal Wave (buy a plastic coat, on sale in the park, to avoid getting soaked on the water rides). These are the park's two most popular rides, so head for them first to save yourself a long wait.

Near by is **Adventure Island**, an outdoor water theme park where the names of the rides tell you what to expect: Tampa Typhoon (a 76-foot/23m free-fall slide), the Gulf Scream speed slide, the Everglides toboggan slide and much more.

Continue north on McKinley Drive to Fowler Avenue. Turn right and head east.

Museum of Science and Industry (MOSI)

9 This is Florida's largest science center featuring over 200 hands-on displays. Favorites include the Gulf Coast Hurricane, where you can be buffeted by 75mph (121km/h) winds in safety; Electric Plaza, which will literally make your hair stand on end; and the Energy Pinball, where you can follow the country's largest pinball through a 700-foot (213m) journey.

Return to the downtown business district.

Exquisite orchids of every hue seduce the eye at the Marie Selby Botanical Gardens

⊡ Sarasota Convention and Visitors Bureau, 655 N Tamiami Trail (**US 41**)

*Head north on **US 41** for 3 miles (5km).*

The Ringling Museums

1 The centerpiece of this magnificent 68-acre (28-hectare) estate is the **John and Mabel Ringling Museum of Art**, one of the finest and largest collections of European paintings in America. The gallery was created in 1927 by John Ringling, who made a fortune in business to add to the circus wealth he created with his brothers. The art collection and the sumptuous Italian Renaissance-style villa in which it is housed have just undergone $18.5 million worth of restoration, and the result is a visual delight. Adjacent is the **Asolo Theatre** complete with an original 18th-century baroque interior. The Ringling Residence, **Ca'd'Zan** (House of John), is a 30-room Venetian Gothic mansion, built in the 1920s tradition of richly decorated historical houses for the wealthy and famous (typified by James Deering's Vizcaya in Miami). Finally, don't miss the **Circus Galleries**, which display a colorful collection of circus art and memorabilia. This exhibit is disappointingly small: one of the reasons is that, surprisingly, Ringling did not include any circus items in his bequest. (Note: admission to the art galleries is always free on Saturday.)

Opposite the Ringling estate is **Bellm Cars and Music of Yesterday**. An entertaining guided tour of the 200-strong antique and classic car collection includes Ringling's Rolls-Royces and Pierce Arrows. You will also be guided around one of the world's largest collections of over 1,100 music machines (barrel organs, nickelodeons, hurdy-gurdies, phonographs, etc) and some of the more interesting examples are played.

Marine life native to the Gulf and Sarasota Bay on display

---

2 days – 168 miles (271km)

SARASOTA & MANATEE COUNTIES

**Sarasota • Ringling Museums • Lido Key
Longboat Key/Anna Maria Key
South Florida Museum • Gamble Plantation
Myakka River State Park • Warm Mineral Springs
Gasparilla Island • Venice
Sarasota**

In 1912 circus magnate John Ringling purchased a large bayfront estate in Sarasota as a winter vacation residence. During the next two decades his appreciation of the arts and his investments had such an impact that the area became a haven for all kinds of artistic talents. Today Sarasota still lays claim to being the cultural capital of the state, with major facilities for opera, ballet, theater and music. Fine dining and exclusive shopping are abundant, but overall prices are sensible and there is little of the elitism of Palm Beach, which Sarasota is sometimes likened to.

Neither is it all culture. There are two beautiful garden attractions here, and an oceanographic institute has pronounced that this area has the finest, whitest sand in the world. The *Marie Selby Botanical Gardens* are among the state's finest; the star attraction is the collection of over 6,000 orchids. Drive 1 mile (1.5km) north to the visitor information center. Adjacent is *Sarasota Quay* and next to this is the bizarre purple seashell shape of the *Van Wezel Hall* which hosts the performing arts.

SCENIC ROUTES

There are no really scenic routes in this area, but **SR 789**, which connects Anna Maria Key southward to Lido Key, guarantees miles of blue-green Gulf water, beaches and some interesting beachfront houses and condominiums.

SPECIAL TO . . .

8 *Gasparilla Island* The southern part of this area is renowned for its fishing. In June and July the best tarpon fishing conditions in the world are found just off Boca Grande Pass.

In late December, early January each year the Ringling Brothers and Barnum and Bailey Circus premiers a new season of shows in its winter home.

Return south on **US 41** *and after Sarasota Quay turn right onto John Ringling Boulevard.*

Lido Key

2 Ringling Causeway leads into St Armand's Circle, a huge traffic circle lined with over a hundred well-heeled fashion, jewelry and specialty stores, plus restaurants and galleries. Continue straight on through the Circle and turn left to Lido Beach, one of the finest in the area. Head back to St Armand's Circle and turn left for **City Island** and the **Mote Marine Science Aquarium**. As well as research projects and a shell exhibit, there are various tanks for marine life, a touch-tank and an outdoor shark tank with several awesome residents in excess of 8 feet (2.4m) and 400 pounds (180kg). Opposite is **The Pelican Man's Bird Sanctuary**, where you can see at work the rehabilitation of birds injured by man.

Return along City Island Road and turn right on **SR 789**.

Longboat Key/Anna Maria Key

3 There is no sightseeing on these barrier islands, but there are good beaches at the northern tip of Longboat Key and on Anna Maria Key, at its southern tip and at the junction

with **SR 64** some 4½ miles (7km) north.

ℹ Anna Maria Chamber of Commerce, 105 39th Street, Holmes Beach; Longboat Key Chamber of Commerce, 510 Bay Isles Road, Sarasota

Follow **SR 64** *east for 12 miles (19km), passing through downtown Bradenton to 10th Street West.*

South Florida Museum and Bishop Planetarium, Bradenton

4 This fine museum traces the area's history with dioramas of the Indian period, a Spanish courtyard and chapel, Cracker accommodation, an outstanding Civil War collection and much more. The star of the museum, however, is Snooty the manatee, who performs more like a sea lion at feeding times. Combined with the museum is **Bishop Planetarium**, with the usual displays plus state-of-the-art laser shows and music.

Continue on 10th Street West, turn north to cross the river and turn right on **US 301**. *Follow this for 3 miles (5km).*

Gamble Plantation State Historic Park

5 Built in the late 1840s using oyster shells and molasses, this is the only pre-Civil War plantation house surviving in south Florida, and until 1856 it was the center of a sugar plantation and refinery covering 3,450 acres (1,396 hectares). Take a ranger-guided tour to see the house, restored and furnished in the style of its heyday.

Continue on **US 301** *to* **I-75**. *Head south to exit 37, then east for 9 miles (14km) on* **SR 72**.

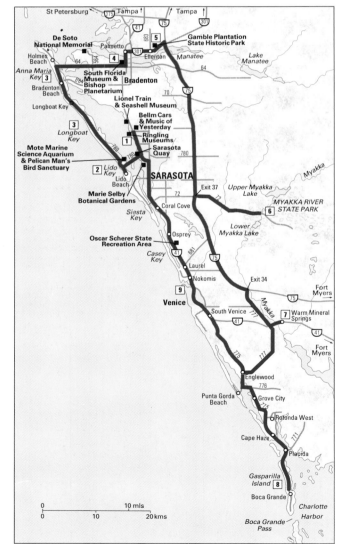

FOR HISTORY BUFFS

4 *Bradenton* In 1539 Hernando de Soto and his conquistadores became the first Europeans to land on this part of Florida. Although the exact site is unknown, the historic event and subsequent explorations are commemorated at the **De Soto National Memorial** a few miles west of Bradenton (north on 75th Street off **SR 64**). There is a visitor center, and costumed guides demonstrate period weapons and tell you about the everyday problems facing the expeditionary force.

In its 14 acres (5.6 hectares) the Marie Selby Botanical Gardens nurture a great range of plants, including these impressive cacti

Myakka River State Park

6 This scenic wildlife sanctuary is similar to the Everglades in places with its grassy marshes and hammocks. You can explore it on foot, by tram tour or aboard the world's largest airboat. Alligators, deer, wild turkeys, hawks and bald eagles are just some of the wildlife you will probably see in this beautiful area.

*Return to **I-75** and head south to exit 34. Take **SR 777** to **US 41** and head east, 21 miles (34km).*

Warm Mineral Springs

7 This is one of the state's most famous 'bottomless' waterholes, where some 10 million US gallons (38 million liters) of water flow daily at a constant 87°F (31°C). The mineral content of the water is claimed to be many times that of more famous spas worldwide, and a health resort has been established on the palm-fringed lake shore.

*Return west on **US 41** for about 1 mile (1.5km) and turn left on **SR 777** to Englewood. At Englewood head south on **SR 775**, which runs into **SR 776** and **SR 771**.*

Gasparilla Island

8 It is said that this barrier island takes its name from José Gaspar (see Tampa), the 18th-century pirate, who used it as a hideout. During the 1920s it was also a popular retreat for more legitimate businessmen such as John Jacob Astor and Henry Du

Pont. They arrived by train, of course, and the railroad station at Boca Grande where they once alighted is now a colorfully converted café-restaurant. The small resort town has changed little in 80 years and the grand **Gasparilla Inn**, built in 1912, still retains a very exclusive guest list. Much of the island is a state recreation area and includes five beaches and an 1890 lighthouse.

*Return to Sarasota on **US 41**, 19 miles (31km).*

Venice

9 This attractive small city, named for its miles of winding waterways, is famous for being the winter home of the Ringling Brothers and Barnum and Bailey Circus and even has a college for trainee clowns. It is also renowned for the number and variety of shark teeth washed up on its shores. Don't be too concerned about swimming here, however, as many of the teeth are fossilized and the likelihood of meeting their owners is very remote.

*Return to Sarasota on **US 41**, 19 miles (31km).*

FOR CHILDREN

Sarasota If Ringling's Circus Gallery and Bellm's cars and music machines are not to their taste, head a little further north on **US 41** to the **Lionel Train and Seashell Museum**. This boasts an extensive working model train layout, plus many coral and shell exhibits.

BACK TO NATURE

Myakka River State Park is a must, but if you would like to see more natural beauty visit **Oscar Scherer State Recreation Area** 2 miles (3km) south of Osprey. Here among the scrubby flatwoods you can fish and canoe in the tidal creek and swim in a freshwater lake.

4 *Bradenton* **Lake Manatee SRA**, 15 miles (24km) east of Bradenton on **SR 64**, has similar character, wildlife and facilities.

RECOMMENDED WALKS

4 *Bradenton* At **De Soto National Memorial Park** a scenic nature trail winds along the Manatee River to the ruins of a house from one of the first settlements in this part of the state, dating back to the 1880s.

6 *Myakka River State Park* Ranger-guided walks are conducted seasonally here.

ORLANDO

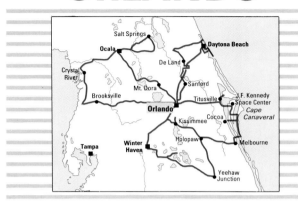

The Orlando area represents the world's most concentrated hive of tourism activity. The key to it all is, of course, Walt Disney World, the home of Mickey Mouse and his supporting cast of thousands. This modern marvel of slick entertainment technology and ebullient, wholesome self-promotion attracts some 25 million visitors annually to the Orlando region. Indeed many tourists head for the magic beacons of Cinderella's Castle and EPCOT Center's great 'golf ball' even before unpacking. You can now quite literally eat, sleep and drink Walt Disney World, and soon transport links will bypass Orlando completely. This is the world's greatest fantasy land and to a large extent sets the tone for most of central Florida's attractions. Step back into the Wild West, join King Henry's Feast, go Back to the Future, visit 11 countries in a day, see all manner of improbable wildlife performing unlikely acts—almost anything is possible here. Thanks also to the need to compete, the standard of non-Disney entertainment is rarely less than highly professional and often quite stunning. There is a downside to this, however. The central parts of Orlando and Kissimmee are characterless, service is conveyor-belt slick and antiseptic, and at certain times of the year you can spend most of a week just waiting in line. It is important to realize, however, that while Walt Disney World is now very much the unofficial symbol of central Florida it is not typical of central Florida.

Just a few minutes' drive from Orlando it is easy to find many vestiges of the old Florida. The area is home to so many hundreds of lakes and dozens of crystal springs that you might be forgiven for thinking it was in danger of sinking. Huge stretches are empty of people and devoted instead to citrus crops, horse breeding and cattle ranching. In these outlying areas bypassed by the gold rush of tourism, small communities and rustic one-horse towns display a wide range of character, from spiritualist to academic, urban sophisticate and wealthy discretion. On the central east coast—the 'Disney coast'—the major resorts provide mostly a cheap and cheerful brand of tourism. There are alternatives and contrasts here too, however. Around the Cape Kennedy area, historic districts and unspoiled nature reserves rub shoulders with one of the greatest displays of high technology ever assembled by man, and there are quiet, understated beach resorts where you can rest far from the crowds of the Magic Kingdom.

The tours covered in this region all start from Orlando, at International Drive.

City Tour 7
Whether or not you explore Orlando, as opposed to just seeing Walt Disney World, is largely a matter of time, money and stamina. However, Disney aside, Orlando does boast some heavyweight attractions. The biggest and best of these are Sea World (which has no Disney counterpart) and Universal Studios. The family nightlife scene is also very lively in Orlando, and a visit to historic Church Street Station is a must for those seeking authentic old-time American entertainment.

Walt Disney World
Old-time, future-time and timeless entertainment of every conceivable kind is served up at Walt Disney World, and rare is the Florida visitor who passes it by. No family should miss it, and even those who profess to prefer the real world to the artificially conceived version will find something to delight them.

Tour 10 and Spaceport USA
After a week of Disney technology, you may feel in need of sand and surf. Take your R and R where the early astronauts did after the high-tech rigors of Cape Canaveral, on the Space Coast beaches. Spaceport USA—the home of the space shuttle—is a good-value day out from Orlando in its own right.

Tour 11
The other most popular choice of coastal break away from Orlando is Daytona Beach. If you like a raucous night scene and think fast wheels are fun, you will probably love it; if you don't, you might easily hate it. Don't let that deter you from visiting the lovely area northwest of Orlando, however. Winter Park is a must for all Orlando visitors, and the Daytona area has several very cultured attractions.

Tour 12
The excursion to Ocala National Forest and Silver Springs features some of Florida's most beautiful woods and river scenery. Silver Springs' glass-bottom boats are every bit as memorable as anything Disney has to offer, with the bonus of being the real thing. There are several other rewarding springs on this route, and those in search of old Florida will not be disappointed.

Tour 13
Old Florida even underlies the final tour, which focuses on the unabashedly tourist-oriented enclave of Kissimmee—though you will have to move away from the neon lights of US 192 to experience it. Just south of here, Cypress Gardens and Bok Tower Gardens are two of the area's most charming and peaceful attractions. Further south, where cattle outnumber people, the theme parks of Orlando seem a world away.

Mickey Mouse, probably the world's most famous cartoon character and official symbol of Walt Disney World, as you have never seen him before, performing 'live' in Specromagic

ORLANDO

Sea World • King Henry's Feast/The Mercado
Fun 'n' Wheels • Wet 'n' Wild • Universal Studios
Church Street Station • Lake Eola Park
Leu Gardens • Loch Haven Park • Sea World

Orlando used to be known as the city that everyone went to and nobody visited. Things have changed since then, but as Walt Disney World continues its seemingly inexorable expansion, Orlando attractions have either had to shape up or be satisfied with the crumbs. Some, like *Sea World* and *Wet 'n' Wild*, have continued to expand and remain at the top of their respective trees; others, like *Church Street Station*, saw a market opportunity (at that time there was no Pleasure Island to satisfy night-revelers); and the most recent major newcomer, *Universal Studios*, is seeking to compete with Disney-MGM Studios head on. Whatever the final outcome, all this rivalry in the tourist industry has certainly benefited vacationers, who have a fantastic choice of things to do and see.

Having a whale of a time at Shamu Stadium in Sea World

Orlando Visitor Information Center, Mercado Mediterranean Village, International Drive

Sea World

1 After Walt Disney World, this is the most visited place in Florida. It also claims to be the most popular marine-life park in the world—and when you see Shamu the 6,000-pound (2,700kg) killer whale leap 6 feet (1.8m) out of the water, you will understand why. Sea World of Florida is one of the four Sea World parks in the US, all of which are dedicated to marine research and educating the public by means of the most entertaining shows and best possible displays of marine life. Spend a full day here and you should be able to see the whole park in relative comfort. The highlights are: Shamu (and Baby Shamu); the sea lion and otter show; **Whale & Dolphin Discovery**, featuring beluga and Pacific black whales; **Terrors of the Deep**, where the world's largest underwater acrylic tunnel will transport you through deadly pufferfish, barracuda, sharks and other fearsome creatures; **Penguin Encounter**, featuring 200 Antarctic penguins in the snow; and the **Tropical Reef**. You can also see Shamu after dark in the spectacular **Night Magic** show and stay on for Sea World's nightly *luau*, a Polynesian revue of exotic dancing, ukuleles, hypnotic war drums, fire jugglers and a South Seas feast.

Take Sea Harbor Drive to International Drive and turn left, heading north.

King Henry's Feast/The Mercado

2 Orlando is big on themed dinner attractions. At King Henry's court you can dig into a five-course 'Olde English' banquet with unlimited beer and wine. Continuous entertainment

Down and down, round and round, in a spin at Wet 'n' Wild

comes in the form of fire eaters, jousting knights, troubadours, jugglers, acrobats and magicians. Across the road at the Mercado shopping village, **Mardi Gras** includes a four-course 'Southern Hospitality' meal and a jazzy two-hour musical revue based on the Mardi Gras and other world festivals. The show is widely applauded, the food is not so hot. Close by is a third International Drive option, the **Plantation Dinner Theatre** at the Heritage Inn.

Continue north on International Drive past Sand Lake Road.

Fun 'n' Wheels

3 This mini-fairground with its four go-kart tracks, bumping boats and cars, water slide, Ferris wheel and much more, will keep kids of all ages amused. Beware the mounting costs, though, as you pay for each ride separately.

Continue north on International Drive and turn right just after Wet 'n' Wild to park your car.

Wet 'n' Wild

4 This is the biggest and most exciting water park in the state,

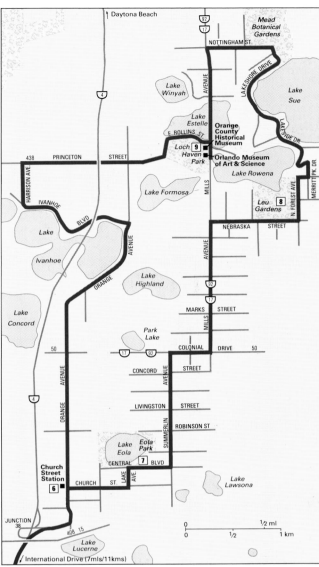

with over a million visitors a year. Every conceivable method of high-speed hydro-sliding is explored here, from riding rapids seated on an inner tube, sledding head-first Cresta-Run fashion on a mat, or simply zooming unassisted through hundreds of feet of twisting, turning, enclosed tubing. Start on the gentler rides and work up to the exhilarating **Black Hole** (a wet version of Space Mountain) and the terrifying-looking **Der Stuka**. This is a breathtaking six-story free-fall onto the world's fastest water slide. Watersports fans can catch a wave at the surf lagoon and try the cable-operated kneeboard rides. There is also a beach here and plenty of other peaceful water activities. (Closed January to mid-February.)

*Continue north on International Drive, past the Elvis Presley Museum on your left to join Kirkman Road (**SR 435**). Go north to Universal Studios.*

Universal Studios

5 This latest Florida theme park is also the largest working film and television studio outside Hollywood. At 444 acres (180 hectares) it is four times the size of its Disney-MGM rival. This does not mean four times

SCENIC ROUTES

The route outlined in the tour between Church Street Station and Loch Haven Park is deliberately chosen for its lake and garden scenery. To continue this drive, head west along East Rollins Street, by the lakeside and turn left onto Camden Road, then onto Princeton Street. Go under I-4, turn left at Harrison Avenue to join Ivanhoe Boulevard (next to Lake Ivanhoe) and pick up Orange Avenue. This heads south back to downtown.

FOR HISTORY BUFFS

Aside from the **Orange County Historical Museum**, which will take you through the development of the area from the time when it was known as Mosquito County, there are no other history exhibits. Visit downtown by day to see little bits of old Orlando still *in situ*—the handsome **Kress Store** and **National Bank** buildings were erected in the 1920s, and the Art Deco-like **McCrory's Five & Dime** actually dates from 1906. The original **Church Street Station** depot has also been renovated and comes complete with an impressive 19th-century steam locomotive.

SPECIAL TO...

There are two regular annual celebrations in town. In early November **Light Up Orlando** is a street carnival with bands, international foods and a celebration of one of its citrus crops, the kumquat. **Arts in April** is a self-explanatory series of visual and performing events. Look out at Church Street Station for festive celebrations, particularly at Halloween and Christmas.

Mel's Diner at Universal Studios

RECOMMENDED WALKS

It is a fair bet that if you have been on your feet all day doing WDW, Sea World or Universal Studios, the last thing you will want to do is to go for a walk. You will certainly have to get away from International Drive, and either **Leu Gardens** or **Turkey Lake Park** is a good choice.

the number of attractions (they have a similar number), but at Universal you can wander around more outdoor sets. The format closely follows Disney's offering of special-effects rides/experiences based on blockbuster films, theater shows illustrating the art of film-making, a tour of the sets and themed restaurants and shopping. Arrive half an hour before official opening time and head for the most popular rides before the lines get really long (waits can take up to two hours). Whatever turns you on is very much a matter of personal taste, and it usually helps if you know the film or television program featured, but these are the big ones: **Back to the Future**—this is probably the most exciting and innovative thrill-ride (a very realistic high-speed simulated chase) currently available and puts even the top Disney thrill-ride, Star Tours, in the shade; **Jaws**—a ride across the lagoon, waiting and watching; **Kong-frontation**, another technical masterpiece based on King Kong; **Earthquake**—good special effects, though lacking a sufficient element of surprise to make it really special. Also recommended are the **Alfred Hitchcock** and **Murder She Wrote** theater shows. **ET** and **Ghostbusters** are comparatively tame and are most popular with children. The **Lagoon Stunt Spectacular** is a confusing babble of flashes and bangs, and the street sets of New York, Hollywood and San Francisco are fun to wander through. Eateries include **The Hard Rock Café** and **Mel's Diner** from *American Graffiti*.

Return south along Kirkman Road and join 1–4 north to exit 38. Turn right onto Orange Avenue and right again onto Church Street.

Church Street Station

6 What was once a crumbling hotel and railroad depot has been brilliantly converted into Orlando's premier evening entertainment complex. The theme basically spans the decades between the 1890s and the Roaring Twenties, and the highlights are the huge three-tiered **Cheyenne Saloon & Opera House**, **Rosie O'Grady's** Louisiana-style bar and the elegant wrought-iron 'crystal palace' **Orchid Garden** (a single

admission price gets you into everything). Antique furnishings and fixtures throughout are of the highest quality, so that each establishment is virtually 'the real thing'. There is music and dancing of every sort, from country and western and the Cheyenne dance team, to Dixieland and can-can girls, bands playing mainstream dance music from the '50s through to the '80s, Phineas Phogg's high-energy disco, and folk and blue-grass when you feel you can do with a mellow moment. Arrive late afternoon or early evening to make sure of seeing all the interesting shops. Eating possibilities are numerous and varied, from the expensive and attractively overblown Lili Marlene's to sandwich bars.

Head east (away from I-4) on either Church Street or South Street (which run parallel at either end of the complex) and turn left onto Lake Avenue.

Lake Eola Park

7 You can rent a swan-shaped paddle boat by day on this picturesque lake or come here by night in a horse and carriage from Church Street Station. Its fountain lit by night and the illuminated backdrop of skyscrapers make an impressive sight.

Head east on Central Boulevard, turn left onto Summerlin Avenue, turn right onto Colonial Drive (US 50) and second left onto Mills Avenue (US 17/92). Turn right onto Nebraska Street, which leads to North Forest Avenue.

Leu Gardens

8 **Leu House** is a restored turn-of-the-century mansion stuffed with artifacts that reflect the lifestyle of the wealthy farmers who cultivated this land between 1910 and 1930. It sits amid 22 acres (9 hectares) of gardens famous for their camellias, roses, orchids and a floral clock.

Continue on North Forest Avenue through Merritt Park, Lakeside and Lakeshore (with lakes on either side of you) to Mead Botanical Gardens on Nottingham Street. This leads back to Mills Avenue. Turn left and soon on your right is Loch Haven Park.

Loch Haven Park

9 This is the center of culture and the arts in Orlando, home to science, art and history galleries. The **Orange County Historical Museum** is a bright, airy place with some excellent re-creations of a general store, a pioneer parlor, a hotel lobby, and much more. Its restored 1926 **Fire Station No 3** holds some interesting antique fire-fighting vehicles. The **Orlando Science Center** features several hands-on exhibits as well as a planetarium that gives daily presentations and weekend laser concerts. The pride of the **Orlando Museum of Art** is its pre-Columbian South American exhibits. The permanent collection also includes 20th-century American and African art.

Return to Sea World (see Scenic Routes).

Spectacular pyrotechnics light the sky above Cinderella's Castle in the best tradition of Walt Disney

WALT DISNEY WORLD

Adventures and Rides

Each park is very different but all feature themed rides or adventures which often involve cinematic special effects (for example, simulation and 3-D techniques) and lifelike animated models. There are very few 'white-knuckle' rides, and these are clearly marked. Among the armory of special effects you will come across are **audio-animatronics** and **Circle-vision**. The former involves extremely realistic robotic models (of either people or animals) that talk or make sounds. Circlevision is a cinematic technique in which a number of projectors and screens are used to surround the viewer (complete surround is referred to as 360-degree Circlevision). The effect is akin to simulation and places you right in the center of the moving action, so that you can see ahead, to both sides and behind you. This is used mostly at **EPCOT Center's World Showcase** where you will 'travel' by train, boat or airplane across the landscapes of many countries.

Magic Kingdom

As Cinderella's Castle rises into view and the strains of *When You Wish Upon a Star* waft through the air, you will realize why this is called the Magic Kingdom. Your introduction to the Kingdom is **Main Street USA**, an idealized re-creation of a turn-of-the-century Main Street in small-town America. The attractions here are mostly shopping, but do pop into the Penny Arcade and don't miss the black-and-white Disney oldies playing continuously at the small cinema.

Mickey Mouse takes a few moments' rest, with young admirers, from a demanding schedule

Now almost synonymous with Florida, the Walt Disney World Resort is the world's leading tourist attraction, boasting over 25 million visits per year. The complex occupies 43 square miles (111sq km)—twice the size of Manhattan Island—and comprises three major theme parks, two water parks, a nature island, a night-time entertainment complex, a shopping village, a campground and 20 resort hotels. The *Magic Kingdom* is the most famous of all the attractions, with Cinderella's Castle and Disney characters bringing back to life all those memories of childhood. This is the place for those who have not yet grown up, but is equally good for those who just don't want to grow up. *EPCOT Center* combines educational and cosmopolitan elements in its attractions while *Disney-MGM Studios* has attractions based on Hollywood in the '50s.

effects are first class. **Big Thunder Mountain**—a runaway train roller-coasters its way through old mining tunnels, a gold-digger's settlement and lots of amusing animatronics. **American Journeys**—a wonderful Circlevision film that takes you coast to coast by plane, helicopter, boat and train. **Jungle Cruise**—an ever-popular gentle 10-minute cruise through waterfalls, jungles, the Nile valley and the African veldt, encountering animatronic elephants, lions, hippos and headhunters.

The best of the rest includes the **Swiss Family Robinson Treehouse** and, in Fantasyland, **It's a Small World** and the 3-D film *Magic Journeys*. The best stage show in the park is the **Diamond Horseshoe Jamboree**, for which you must book seats at the Hospitality House on Main Street (do this as soon as you arrive in the morning). Daily events include the Three O'clock Parade, a carnival procession, and when park hours are extended, the **Spectromagic Parade**, a carnival by night with spectacular lights, lasers and special effects.

EPCOT Center

The Experimental Prototype Community of Tomorrow—EPCOT Center for short—was conceived in 1966 by Walt Disney as a real-life multinational community. Although it

---

Left: Visitors ride the Big Thunder Mountain Railroad in Frontierland

---

Below: Sleek conveyance astride the monorail at Future World. Spaceship Earth sits golf ball-like beyond

You will need at least two days to see the Magic Kingdom, the same for EPCOT, and one day for Disney-MGM, so if you can afford it, a **five-day Super Pass** is a good investment (the pass includes admission to the three parks and all attractions described previously except Pleasure Island).

If you intend doing all three parks, see EPCOT first, then Disney-MGM, and leave the Magic Kingdom until last, particularly if you have children. For them (and also for many grown-ups) the Magic Kingdom is a very hard act to follow.

Besides Main Street, there are other themed 'lands' within the park— **Adventureland, Frontierland, Fantasyland, Tomorrowland** and **Liberty Square**—containing over 100 attractions. Fantasyland (including **Mickey's Starland**) is geared for young children, and Tomorrowland leans toward the future. The following are the main showpiece attractions: **Space Mountain**—this roller coaster in the dark is something of a theme park legend and is the only truly hair-raising ride in the Magic Kingdom. **Pirates of the Caribbean**—a boat ride through a series of sets depicting a port being sacked by pirates, is Disney animatronics at their best. The **Haunted Mansion** —frightening it isn't, but the special

proved impractical, the **Future World** section of EPCOT still retains one of the original objectives of 'showing off the latest US technologies and the imagination of free enterprise'. Here the emphasis is less on rides for thrills than rides for learning. The highlights of Future World are: **Universe of Energy**—three films and an ingenious moving theater ride take you through 'the forces that fuel our lives', from animatronic dinosaurs to a thunderous space shuttle launch on a 220-degree movie screen.

Wonders of Life—an exciting simulator thrill ride (Body Wars), an Animatronic show (Cranium Command) plus a humorous and sensitive movie (The Making of Me).

Captain EO (in Journey into

Imagination pavilion)—a 17-minute George (*Star Wars*) Lucas film starring Michael Jackson, with incredible 3-D effects.

Listen to the Land (in The Land pavilion)—a cruise through various world climes to see how agriculture may look in the future.

The **Living Seas**—the centerpiece of this sea-life exhibit is the world's largest man-made saltwater tank, with over 80 species of tropical fish and mammals.

In addition, car lovers will enjoy **The World of Motion**, and curiosity alone may demand a ride into the landmark silver geospheric 'golf ball' that is the symbol of EPCOT and hosts **Spaceship Earth**. The lines are usually long, but many rate this attraction highly.

The other half of EPCOT Center is **World Showcase**, which resembles a permanent World Fair. Here 11 countries have done a remarkable job of transforming part of Florida into the buildings, sights, sounds, smells and tastes of a foreign country. Each pavilion has its own architectural showpiece (from a Mayan pyramid to the Eiffel Tower), shops and at least one restaurant—in fact there is a surfeit of culinary excellence here, in contrast to the poverty of the more ordinary fare in the Magic Kingdom.

The United States, Norway, Mexico, China, France and Canada also feature a ride and/or a striking Circlevision film, while entertainment is often provided outside the pavilions by national street performers, who range from folk dancers and comedy players to bagpipers and Oriental drummers. Don't miss Mexico, China, Japan, Morocco, France and Canada.

The end of every day at EPCOT Center is celebrated in the most breathtaking fashion by Illuminations, a pyrotechnic extravaganza of lights, lasers, fountains and music that is truly amazing, even by Disney standards.

Disney-MGM Studios

Hollywood Boulevard replaces Main Street USA, the theme tune from *Gone With the Wind* takes the place of *When You Wish Upon a Star*, and Harrison Ford takes the starring role from Peter Pan in this magic kingdom for film lovers. If you have already seen the other Disney theme parks, you will know what to expect in terms of animatronics, rides and special effects. This is also a genuine working studio, and the best possible introduction is to take the excellent two-hour **Backstage Studio Tour**, which gives an insight into what goes on behind the scenes. If your tram survives the special effects of Catastrophe Canyon, you will be shown a host of other mechanical and optical tricks of the trade, cleverly exposed by first watching an amusing and calamitous short film starring Bette Midler, then examining its props and special-effects equipment at first hand. To see how cartoons of all kinds are created, take the equally dynamic **Animation Tour** featuring a brilliant Robin Williams/Walter Cronkite short film. Other favorites of

Right: Action in the Indiana Jones Stunt Spectacular

this studio are **Star Tours**, the **Indiana Jones Epic Stunt Spectacular** and **Jim Henson's Muppet Vision 3D**. The former vies with Space Mountain as the fastest, most thrilling Disney ride. This one, however, is a space flight simulation, created by George Lucas, and has all the excitement of actually being inside the cockpit of a *Star Wars* craft during a hair-raising, hyperspeed adventure. The Indiana Jones Stunt Spectacular is a live production on a huge stage with our hero (actually a Ford look-alike) re-enacting some of the most heart-stopping scenes from the blockbuster movies. On the central park backlot, the Muppets appear for an on-location film shoot, and a courtyard away is the Jim Henson's Muppet Vision 3-D, a combination of 'live' Muppets and 3-D film antics. There is lots more to see here, including two audience participation shows, one demonstrating sound effects (**The Monster Sound Show**), the other showing the craft of television production (**Superstars TV**); an American TV game show *(Let's Make a Deal)* and a walk-through adventure based on *Honey, I Shrunk the Kids*. Largest of all Disney's ride-through attractions is **The Great Movie Ride**, which reproduces some of the greatest moments in film history. Nostalgia is also a key element in the legendary **Hollywood Brown Derby**, which serves as the studio's flagship restaurant. Finally, during the summer the **Sorcery in the Sky** fireworks show ends the day in style.

Below: Face to face with Alien on the Great Movie Ride

PRACTICAL TIPS

The least crowded seasons are January through the first week in February, September through November (except Thanksgiving weekend) and from Thanksgiving to the beginning of the Christmas vacation. Post-Easter through early June is also a relatively light season. Although there is a special magic to Walt Disney World at Christmas, it is not worth making your first trip at this or any other peak period if you want to avoid very long lines. However, even at the quietest times you will still encounter lengthy waits for the more popular attractions. The basic strategy to beat the crowds (or at least to attempt to) is, first, to arrive at the park entrance well before the gates open. Then head straight for the furthest point, picking out the most popular rides in the park, and work your way back towards the entrance. Make the most of late opening hours in summer as well. Surprisingly, the busiest days are Monday, Tuesday and Wednesday (Thursday is also often busy at Disney-MGM).

Pleasure Island

This vibrant evening entertainment complex covers 6 acres (2.4 hectares) and takes in six nightclubs, the *Empress Lilly* steamboat, various restaurants, shops and a movie theater complex. A single admission will get you into all clubs and you can actually do all six in one night if you arrive by around 9pm, although it is a little tiring and three is more sensible. The clubs are open until 2am nightly, and there is a 'New Year's Eve Street Party' every night. Persons under 21 must be accompanied by a parent.

Both the **Comedy Warehouse** and **The Adventurers Club** are comedy clubs. The first is a fairly conventional offering, though no less funny for that; the second is a 1930s-style travelers' club, where talking animal heads look down from the wall and you are ushered into the club's 'private library' for a show featuring tall tales. The **Neon Armadillo** features live country and blue-grass, music and **XZFR** (pronounced Zephyr) **Rock & Roll Beach Club** hosts live bands playing oldies and recent rock dance standards. **Mannequins Dance Palace** is a high-energy state-of-the-art disco, complete with a touch of Disney magic, that could hold its own on the nightclub circuit of any major metropolis. The final choice is **Cage**, featuring Top 40 music videos. (Note: you must be 21 or older to enter Cage and Mannequins.)

Typhoon Lagoon and River Country

River Country came first, designed as the idyllic Huckleberry Finn-style swimmin' hole, with rope swings, slides and flumes. The whole area is beautifully landscaped (complete with a lovely white-sand beach) and is also good for swimming. Typhoon Lagoon, four times the size of River

Body surfers catch the wave at Typhoon Lagoon

Country, is probably the world's most innovative water theme park, with the typical Disney eye for fantasy detail and immaculate landscaping. Thrilling water slides and rapids rides spew out from a towering mountain topped by a stranded pirate galleon, but perhaps best of all is the amazing inland body-surfing lagoon (the world's largest), where you can catch 6-foot (1.8m) waves. A Caribbean reef offers snorkeling among exotic fish and, again, a perfect beach. Lines for the slides can be long; the best times to visit are Monday, Tuesday and Friday, or Sunday morning.

Discovery Island

This beautifully landscaped zoological island is the perfect retreat when you have had enough of crowds, lines, animatronics and thrill rides. Nature trails and walk-through aviaries feature parrots, monkeys, flamingos, alligators and giant tortoises in natural habitats—altogether some 90 animal species and 250 plant species spread over 11 acres (4.5 hectares).

PRACTICAL TIPS

Walt Disney World has several resort hotels within its boundaries, each with its own theme. They range from the moderately priced Port Orleans, which opened in June last year, and the Caribbean Beach, up to the deluxe Grand Floridian. Also relatively new are the Yacht and Beach Club resorts, within walking distance of EPCOT Center. Recently opened in January was Dixie Landings, giving guests a taste of Louisiana. The Contemporary Hotel and Polynesian Resort both have monorail access to the Magic Kingdom and EPCOT Center.

PRACTICAL TIPS

To make sure of a table at any of the international restaurants in EPCOT's World Showcase, you must make a reservation either in advance or as soon as you enter the park on one of the computer terminals at Earth Station.

A frenzied party reaches its zenith as midnight strikes on Pleasure Island

Cocoa Beach has many ocean front hotels, bars and restaurants to complement its miles of white sand

ⓘ Orlando Visitor Information Center, Mercado Mediterranean Village, International Drive

*From Orlando take **I-4** north to exit 41 and head west for 40 miles (64km) on **SR 50**, crossing **I-95**, to the Indian River/ Intracoastal Waterway. Turn left onto **US 1** and head north for 4 miles (6km). Turn right to cross the river on **SR 402**.*

Merritt Island National Wildlife Refuge

1 Adjacent to Spaceport USA, this barrier island is an unspoiled wilderness stretching 25 miles (40km), home to 22 endangered and threatened species. At the Visitor Contact Point pick up a leaflet detailing the **Black Point Wildlife Drive**, a self-guided drive routed through areas of wading birds and other waterfowl. Take any of the three walking trails and you might see some of the refuge's land animals, including armadillo, deer, wild pigs, otters and turtles. The best times for viewing are early morning and late afternoon between October and March. Another option, renting a canoe, may get you up close to a manatee. The Canaveral National Seashore is one of the state's most untouched beaches. At the southern end, **Playalinda** is good for swimming and surfing, but to the north you are just as likely to see giant loggerheads and green turtles as other humans.

*Return to and follow **US 1** south for 8 miles (13km), then turn right onto NASA Parkway West (**SR 405**) to the Space Center Executive Airport.*

Valiant Air Command Museum

2 This was the operations center and headquarters for the Valiant Air Command during World War II. It is now dedicated to preserving and restoring World War II and post-war military aircraft and displays them along with war memorabilia.

Head back east to enter the NASA JFK Space Center by Gate 3.

US Space Camp

3 If you have ever wondered what 'the right stuff' really is and whether or not you have got it, this will go some way towards telling you. After seeing the film footage, space memorabilia and personal items belonging to such pioneers as John Glenn and Alan Shepard, you can experience some of their training methods firsthand. Take a moon walk in the one-sixteenth gravity chair, try out the *2001*-style Manned Maneuvering Unit and repair a satellite aboard the Five Degrees of Freedom simulator. You will also hear unreleased tapes of astronauts' conversations.

Merritt Island National Wildlife Refuge, home to migratory waterfowl

THE SPACE COAST

Orlando ● Merritt Island National Wildlife Refuge
Valiant Air Command Museum
US Space Camp ● Port Canaveral
Cocoa Village ● Cocoa Beach ● Eau Gallie
Melbourne ● Orlando

The Space Coast has two great attributes: it features the closest beaches to Walt Disney World and it is home to the John F Kennedy Space Center, otherwise known as Spaceport USA. If you are staying in the Orlando area, it would be a shame to miss *Spaceport USA*, which is undoubtedly one of the wonders of the technological world. Even if the technicalities of space travel leave you cold, you will find the sheer scale of the hardware on display and the achievement of the explorers who have been launched from this site quite extraordinary. Moreover, given that a whole day here costs much less than an equivalent day sightseeing in Orlando, it is hard to dispute Spaceport's claim that it is indeed the best visitor value in the state. The beaches also offer good value for money, with prices here among the lowest in peninsular Florida. Compared to the west coast resorts, however, Cocoa Beach has little to offer. It is certainly the best bet for a day out at the beach, but for a longer stay some may find it rather quiet. However, if peace and quiet are what you crave after Walt Disney World, then the natural appeal of Merritt Island and the understated elegance of historic Cocoa Village and old Melbourne have much to offer.

SPACEPORT USA

After the establishment of NASA (the National Aeronautics and Space Administration) in 1958, the early manned space missions, Mercury and Gemini, were launched from Cape Canaveral Air Force Station. In 1964 the NASA Kennedy Space Center headquarters was relocated a short distance away to its present home on Merritt Island. Following the historic Apollo missions the focus is now on the reusable space shuttle which can be sent into orbit time and time again.

Touring the site
Because this is an operational site, access outside the main visitor complex (the **Galaxy Center**) is strictly limited to bus tours. These are extremely popular, so as soon as you arrive book tickets for the Red Bus Tour (and also the **IMAX** theater). There are two bus tours (both lasting two hours), which depart regularly throughout the day. The **Red Tour** will show you Apollo mission and space shuttle sites, while the **Blue Tour** takes you to Cape Canaveral to see the pioneer space sites. If this is your first visit the Red Tour is recommended. Stops are quite frequent (operations permitting) and include an authentic re-creation of the Apollo launch control firing room and the first lunar landing by Apollo 11 in 1969. A photo stop by the incredible and aptly named **Giant Crawler Shuttle Transporter** brings you right up to date. Weighing about 3,000 US tons (over 2,700 metric tons), this giant platform on four caterpillar tracks rumbles along at 1 mph (1.6km/h) transporting the shuttle from the Vehicle Assembly Building (VAB) the $3\frac{1}{2}$ miles (5.5km) to the launch pad. Tourists cannot enter the VAB, but as it is one of the world's biggest buildings, you cannot help but see it. The final giant that you will stop alongside is **Saturn V**: this rocket, which carried the Apollo missions to the moon, is the largest and most powerful ever built in the US. It measures 363 feet (111m) long and weighs 31,000 US tons (over 28,000 metric tons). The only disappointment about the tour is that, for security reasons, you never get very close to the space shuttle or launch pad and, at two hours, it is often too long for young children.

The Galaxy Center
The highlight of the center is the **IMAX** movie theater, which shows two films, 'The Dream Is Alive' and 'Blue Planet'. IMAX is a special, very

Not horticultural but astronautical: the Rocket Garden is never less than awe-inspiring

large-scale cinema technique that takes you right into the picture almost as a simulator would. The screen is a massive five stories high, and when the space shuttle blasts off in 'The Dream Is Alive' you will feel the vibrations and experience the awesome power almost as if you were there. Parts of this were shot by the astronauts while living in space, and if you can only see one of the two IMAX films, this one is recommended. However, there is plenty more to see in the Galaxy Center, and at no extra cost. The **Gallery of Space Flight** features actual space hardware from many missions including Gemini and Apollo space suits, models and all kinds of paraphernalia; 'The Boy from Mars' is a fictional film about a space

colony; the **Spaceport Theater** shows changing films; **Satellites and You** is a 55-minute journey through a future space station complete with robotic spacemen. Outside is the famous 'rocket park', where a number of historic craft are proudly displayed pointing skywards, while the striking **Astronauts' Memorial** attests to the perils of space travel.

Allow five to six hours for your visit. To see if a shuttle is due for launch phone NASA before visiting, on (800) 432-2153 (toll free). Launches are a great sight but very often are delayed (sometimes for days), and they inevitably mean large crowds and restricted access to the site.

*Rejoin the Space Coast tour by turning south onto Kennedy Parkway South (**SR 3**) and leave the NASA complex by Gate 2. After 2 miles (3km) turn left onto Bennett Causeway.*

BACK TO NATURE

The opportunities to get close to nature are abundant on this relatively undeveloped coast. Merritt Island is a completely unspoiled nature-lover's paradise, while the Brevard Museum provides an urban wildlife sanctuary. Look for herons, ibises, waders, terns and gulls. You can also take an airboat ride along the St John's River to see wild alligators and elegant cypress trees. The station is at **Lone Cabbage Fish Camp** on SR 520, 4 miles (6km) west of **I-95**.

FOR HISTORY BUFFS

5 *Cocoa Village* Walking tours of historic Cocoa Village are conducted on a regular basis (ask at the Chamber of Commerce). The **Porcher House** on Delannoy Avenue is open to the public 10 am to 1 pm Tuesday through Friday. Built in 1916 in Classic Revival style, it has recently been renovated. The Porcher family was once the county's largest citrus grower.

RECOMMENDED WALKS

Merritt Island National Wildlife Refuge offers three walking trails. The **Oak Hammock** is a ½-mile (800m) trail through a subtropical forest, while the **Palm Hammock** includes boardwalks and stretches for 2 miles (3km). The **Cruickshank** circles a shallow-water marsh, and its observation tower is ideal for bird-watching.

SCENIC ROUTES

In addition to the Black Point Wildlife Drive on Merritt Island, the routes directly along the Indian River are recommended. Take **SR 515**, which runs parallel to **US 1** for 16 miles (26km), starting some 4 miles (6km) south of Kennedy Space Center Gate 3. The **Tropical Trail**, on the other side of the river, runs parallel to **SR 3** and can be reached by making a right turn off **SR 3** (heading south) some 2½ miles (4km) south of the Bennett Causeway (**SR 528**).

Port Canaveral

4 You can visit here simply to admire the big boats that dock at this important cruise terminal, or you could take one of Florida's famous 'cruises to Nowhere'. Choose from SeaEscape (see also Miami, Fort Lauderdale and St Petersburg) or EuropaSun. SeaEscape also cruises to the Bahamas, as does the Premier Cruise Line, the latter complete with assorted Walt Disney characters.

Drive south on SR A1A for 3 miles (5km) and turn right onto SR 520. Continue west for 2½ miles (4km) and cross the causeway.

Cocoa Village

5 Historic Cocoa Village is a delight, a Victorian block of around 50 shops and restaurants, the earliest dating back to the 1880s, when the official population here numbered just 25. On Delannoy Avenue is Travis Hardware, built in 1907 and still operated by the same family. The original tin ceiling remains, as do the track ladders used to reach merchandise on the higher shelves.

A mile (1.5km) west on SR 520 at Brevard Community College is the **Astronaut Memorial Hall**. There is a small museum here, but the real attraction is its planetarium, where you can explore the universe through Florida's largest public telescope. Laser shows are staged on Friday and Saturday nights (everything closed Sunday). Currently under development, the planetarium will be one of the biggest complexes in the world when complete. Close by, on Michigan Avenue, is the **Brevard Museum of History and Natural Science**. Exhibits include a large shell collection, pioneer antiques, a children's Discovery Room and nature trails that explore a 22-acre (9-hectare) nature preserve.

☐ Cocoa Chamber of Commerce, Sunbank Building, King Street

From Cocoa Village cross back over the bridge on SR 520, through Merritt Island and turn right on SR A1A heading south.

Cocoa Beach

6 There isn't a great deal to this traditional resort aside from its good, gently shelving beaches which are popular with families. **Canaveral Pier**, with various facilities, extends 800 feet (244m) into the Atlantic, but the most striking landmark is the alarmingly gaudy **Ron Jon Surf Shop**. At the southern end of the beach is **Patrick Air Force Base** missile test center. From the road you can see a smaller version of the Spaceport USA rocket park, except that these were once deadly missiles.

☐ Cocoa Beach Area Chamber of Commerce, Fortenberry Road, Merritt Island (Chamber of Commerce also on SR A1A)

Continue for another 2½ miles (4km) south and turn right onto the Eau Gallie Causeway (SR 518). Cross the river and take the second right, Highland Avenue.

Experience Florida's coastal wilderness, with its abundant wildlife at home in the dunes and lagoons of Canaveral National Seashore

Eau Gallie

7 This historic suburb of the town of Melbourne holds two fine attractions. Park at the **Brevard Art Center and Museum**. This large, attractive modern facility is renowned for its touring exhibitions from collections of national stature. Gallery tours are given in the afternoon, Tuesday through Friday. Across the street is the **Space Coast Science Center**. If you have ever wondered what a dinosaur egg feels like, how freeze-dried astronaut food tastes or what 'a million' really looks like, there are some 30 hands-on stations plus visiting exhibits to help you learn (closed Sunday).

*Turn left past the Science Center onto St Clair Street and then left onto Harbor City Boulevard (**US 1**). Continue for 3 miles (5km) to the junction with New Haven Avenue (**US 192**).*

Melbourne

8 The historic turn-of-the-century heart of Melbourne lies along **Crane Creek**. Here you will find many restored shops, galleries and restaurants. These include **Nannie Lee's Strawberry Mansion** (on East New Haven Avenue/Strawbridge Avenue). Built in 1905, this was a social, religious and civic meeting house until its recent conversion into a restaurant. At the scenic harbor a few blocks away, you can sometimes see dolphins and manatees in the protected waterway.

*Return to Orlando via Kissimmee on **US 192**, a distance of (72 miles 116km).*

Orlando–Merritt Island **56 (90)**
Merritt Island–Valiant Air Command Museum **9 (14)**
Valiant Air Command Museum–US Space Camp **2 (3)**
US Space Camp–Port Canaveral **23 (37)**
Port Canaveral–Cocoa Village **10 (16)**
Cocoa Village–Cocoa Beach **10 (16)**
Cocoa Beach–Eau Gallie **16 (26)**
Eau Gallie–Melbourne **3 (5)**
Melbourne–Orlando **72 (116)**

SPECIAL TO ...

8 *Melbourne* The 12-mile (19km) stretch of sand south between Melbourne Beach and Sebastian Inlet is the largest sea turtle nesting area in the US. Under cover of night between May and October, endangered turtles clamber out onto the sands to lay as many as 120 leathery eggs, each the size of a ping-pong ball. You can take guided walks to watch the turtles at Merritt Island National Wildlife Refuge (June–August), and Sebastian Inlet State Recreation Area (June–July). Ask at any chamber of commerce for more details, and make reservations as far in advance as possible.

FOR CHILDREN

If the high-tech world of space exploration or the Space Coast Science Center fails to please, try the natural world at **Gator Jungle**, 6 miles (10 km) west of **Titusville** on East Highway (**SR 50**). This is claimed to be the largest alligator farm in Florida, with over 10,000 crocs and 'gators raised for their meat and skins. You can see them in their natural habitat aboard a **Jungle Cruise**. Several other species of wildlife are also kept within the 20-acre (8-hectare) farm.

3 days – 191 miles (307km)

WINTER PARK TO DAYTONA BEACH

Orlando • Rollins College
Park Avenue/Morse Gallery of Art
Sanford Zoo • Blue Springs State Park
Cassadaga • De Land • De León Springs
The Casements • Birthplace of Speed Museum
Halifax Historical Museum • Daytona Beach
Ponce de León Inlet • Sugar Mill Gardens
Daytona Museum of Arts and Sciences
Daytona International Speedway • Orlando

The area covered by this route is difficult to characterize. It is not a recognized geographical area, and the two communities featured at either end of it—Winter Park and Daytona—are as different as day and night. It is highly unlikely that devotees of 'Little Europe' would care to be caught dead on 'the world's most famous beach', and vice-versa! However, a day out at lively Daytona will at least put a face to the famous name, and if the college kids are raising hell on the beach, there is plenty of alternative cultural and historic interest close at hand. In fact, between the bustle of Orlando and Daytona, peace and calm are the rule. If you are considering Daytona for your second week, you may enjoy getting there slowly. There are no more relaxing spots in all of Florida than Blue Springs and De León Springs, and in communities such as Cassadaga and De Land you will find vestiges of the old Florida.

RECOMMENDED WALKS

The Winter Park lakes are a lovely place to stretch your legs, so too is the campus of Rollins College. The Stetson University campus at De Land is equally pleasant, and there are plenty of short nature walks available in the Daytona area. Try Sugar Mill Gardens, Tomoka State Park, Ponce de León Inlet Lighthouse area or the Ormond Beach Memorial Art Gallery grounds.

☑ Orlando Visitor Information Center, Mercado Mediterranean Village, International Drive

From Orlando take I-4 north to exit 45. Turn right and follow Fairbanks Avenue east for nearly 2 miles (3km). At the seventh intersection after crossing US 17-92, Park Avenue, turn right on Holt Avenue, then left into the Rollins College campus.

Rollins College/Cornell Fine Arts Museum

1 This delightful collection is one of central Florida's hidden treasures. Its outstanding paintings vary from works by Renaissance, baroque and European old masters through 19th-

Daytona Beach: the cars are out of sight, if not out of mind

century and contemporary American artists. Elsewhere in the museum Native American artifacts from the Southwest, Chippendale furniture and Tiffany glass rub shoulders in harmony. Here, at Florida's oldest college, you are free to wander the elegant campus. You can see more of the lovely wooded grounds by taking a lake boat tour. This is also an excellent way of viewing the homes of some of Winter Park's millionaires.

Return to Park Avenue.

Park Avenue/Morse Gallery of Art

2 Leafy Park Avenue, lined with European-style shops, fine restaurants, hidden gardens and antique and art galleries, is often called the most beautiful shopping street in central Florida. The jewel in its crown is the Morse Gallery of Art on East Welbourne Avenue. This intimate museum features the biggest and finest collection of the works of Louis Tiffany, world-famous for his Art Nouveau glass. Tiffany lamps, paintings, pottery, metalwork and furniture are also displayed, complemented by contemporary works of masters like Frank Lloyd Wright and Charles Rennie Mackintosh.

Continue north on Park Avenue and turn right onto Orlando Avenue (US 17–92). Continue north across SR 436 heading towards I-4, exit 52.

Sanford Zoo

3 This relatively small but important zoo is home to hundreds of birds and animals. You will see cougar, siamangs, serval and margay and hear the laughing Australian kookaburra. Go at the weekend if possible to see the public feeding of the primates, hippos, otters and felines. Sanford's other big attraction is the 1800s-style *Grand Romance* riverboat (reservations required). You can take a dinner-dance cruise or just go sightseeing along the scenic St John's River. To find the marina at Monroe Harbor, return south, turn left onto SR 46 and at the fourth light turn left.

From the zoo continue north on US 17-92 for 9 miles (14km). At Orange City turn left on West French Avenue and head 2 miles (3km) west.

Blue Springs State Park

4 This peaceful state park is famous as a winter home for manatees, who seek refuge from the cold St John's River in the warm waters here—a constant 72°F (22°C). There is an observation platform, and from it you can usually see these gentle giants from November through March (February is particularly good). Once a river port, the park presents its history in an 1870s mansion.

Return to Orange. City. Head north on US 17-92 for a short distance, turn right, then left, crossing I-4. Follow the signs to Cassadaga.

The exquisite work of Louis Tiffany at the Morse Gallery

Cassadaga

5 This tiny backwoods community is famous for being Florida's spiritualist center. Wandering around the village you will find that a number of mediums advertize their services, available on a walk-in basis, or you can just visit the **Purple Rose Metaphysical Stuff Store**. There is nothing remotely spooky about Cassadaga, and the picturesque diversion gives a glimpse of old Florida.

Continue north and then west in a loop back to **US 17-92** *via Lake Helen, and head north for 3 miles (5km).*

De Land

6 The **University of Stetson** is the major feature of this charming quiet town, and visitors are welcome to look around the campus with its handsome porticos and pillars. **DeLand Hall**, facing the main street, dates back to 1884 and is the state's oldest building in continuous use for higher education. Across the road is the modern **Cultural Arts Center**, which houses the **DeLand Museum of Art**. Just off the main street, on West Michigan Avenue, is the **Henry Addison DeLand House**. You can tour this delightful property dating from the 1890s and see memorabilia relating to the city's founder.

Continue north on **US 17** *for 9 miles (14km).*

De León Springs

7 A major spring, naturally pumping 19 million US gallons (72 million liters) of water each day, this is a wonderful place for swimming and canoeing. A highlight of the park is the picturesque **Old Mill**, now a restaurant, complete with its huge wooden wheel, which once worked a Spanish sugar mill. Each table has its own griddle, and patrons are given a pitcher of batter, plus toppings, to create their own pancakes.

Continue north for 6 miles (10km) to Barberville and turn right. Head east on **SR 40** *for 24 miles (39km). Cross the Ormond Bridge onto East Granada Boulevard and turn immediately right onto Riverside Drive.*

The Casements

8 This sturdy handsome wooden house, named after its numerous casement windows, was built in the early 1900s and from 1918 to 1937 was the winter home of Standard Oil billionaire John D Rockefeller. It is now a cultural and civic center, but tours are given of several rooms restored to Rockefeller's era (closed Sunday). The top floor features, unexpectedly, a museum of Hungarian folk art full of colorful national costumes and an equally unlikely Boy Scout exhibit. The house is elegant but very modest for a man of Rockefeller's massive wealth and was a great source of friction with his family, who declined to visit such a humble abode. Rockefeller moved to Ormond Beach for health reasons and spent his first two winters at the Ormond Hotel, a typically grand Henry Morrison Flagler structure, built in 1888. Local legend has it that he moved to The Casements, opposite the hotel, after he discovered he was being deliberately overcharged because of his wealth. The Ormond, long since closed, now stands semiderelict and its future is uncertain. A block away, on East Granada Boulevard, is the **Ormond Memorial Art Gallery and Garden**, featuring lush tropical grounds.

Walk or drive two blocks east.

SCENIC ROUTES

A lakeside drive around Winter Park is highly recommended. Head west on Fairbanks Avenue into Osceola, left onto Genius Drive, right onto Mizell Avenue, left onto Lakemont, left again onto Bryan, skirting Lake Osceola, then north to the east side of Lake Maitland and back towards Park Avenue. The first half of Riverside Drive, alongside the Halifax River in Ormond Beach looking over toward The Casements, is also very picturesque.

FOR HISTORY BUFFS

7 *De León Springs* Close to Barberville is the **Pioneer Settlement for the Creative Arts**. This is a living history museum where costumed interpreters give demonstrations of spinning, weaving, candle-making and many other aspects of pioneer life (closed Sunday). Aviation enthusiasts may like to see an impressive full-size stainless steel replica of the Wright Flyer, the world's first sustained and controlled powered aircraft. It is located in front of the **Aeronautical University** off Clyde Morris Boulevard, south of Volusia Avenue.

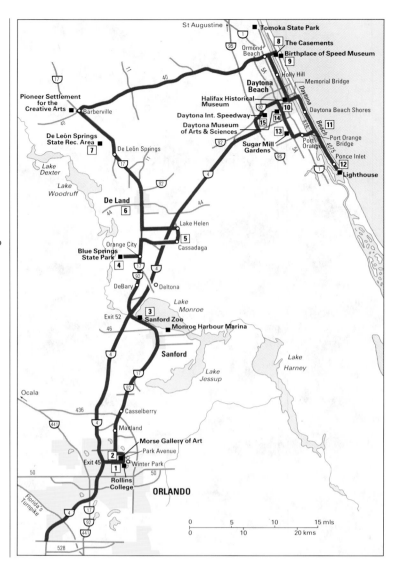

BACK TO NATURE

11 *Daytona Beach* Any of the fine state parks or recreation areas on this route are recommended. The nearest to Daytona is **Tomoka State Park**, 3 miles (5km) north of Ormond Beach, at the confluence of the Tomoka and Halifax rivers. In addition to nature trails you can take a boat trip or the 16-mile (26km) canoe trail to explore the lovely Tomoka River.

Birthplace of Speed Museum

9 The Daytona Beach area has been known as the speed capital of the world since 1902, when the likes of Henry Ford and R E Olds (of Oldsmobile fame) raced along the compacted sand at the death-defying speed of 57mph (92km/h). Two years later the *Stanley Steamer* reached 197mph (315km/h) just before writing itself off in spectacular fashion (the driver was unhurt). Since then the greatest speed on earth has been reached 14 times on the Daytona/Ormond sands, one of the most famous occasions being in 1935, when Sir Malcolm Campbell reached 276mph (444km/h) in *Bluebird*. You can see a replica of the *Stanley Steamer* and other record-breaking machines in the museum. However, considering the city's great racing heritage, this is a disappointingly small collection and will probably appeal only to speed aficionados.

Return across Ormond Bridge and turn immediately left onto South Beach Street. Continue for 4½ miles (7km).

Halifax Historical Museum

10 Step back and admire the splendid Classicist façade of the **Merchants Bank** building that houses the museum. Built in 1910, the bank lasted just 19 years before succumbing to the Great Depression. The museum (closed Sunday) is a small but interesting collection of historical exhibits and records relating to Volusia County. These range from a 600-year-old Timucuan Indian canoe and Spanish artifacts salvaged from plantation ruins, through to the early

The fishing pier at Daytona Beach, near a wide and popular promenade

years of beach racing. You can look through a complete newspaper file dating back to 1883 and see a 1909 time capsule.

*After Memorial Bridge take the first left turn and continue along Silver Beach Avenue to South Atlantic Avenue (**SR A1A**).*

Daytona Beach

11 They call this the world's most famous beach in honor of its record-breaking speed legacy, but these days the 23 miles (37km) of compacted white shoreline usually resemble a huge parking lot. If you prefer beaches without internal combustion engines, this is a place to avoid. But if you want to drive on the hallowed sands, you will have to pay for the privilege—and with a speed limit of 10mph (16km/h) you won't be setting any records. Proximity to Walt Disney World and cheap accommodations attract families on a tight budget, regular motorcycle racing attracts hordes of leather-clad bikers, and each spring break thousands of college revelers turn the town into one giant raucous party. The beachfront is a depressing line of cheap bars and downmarket motels. On the bright side, the recently renovated **Pier**, claimed to be the longest on the whole of America's East Coast, is a good place for children, and the **Ocean Center** features good-quality live family entertainment shows.

Continue south.

Ponce de León Inlet

12 As the cheap hotels subside, Ponce de León Inlet begins. This altogether more pleasant stretch of coastline ends after some 5 miles (8km) at the **Ponce de León Inlet Lighthouse**. The lighthouse, built in 1887 and towering 175 feet (53m), is

the centerpiece of a small museum complex. Dark for many years, the lighthouse was relit in 1982 and is once again active. After scaling the 203 steps, visit the museums in the keeper's and assistant's cottages, a restored 1890s cottage and various other outbuildings.

*Continue along Beach Street, turn right onto South Peninsula Drive and head back in a loop onto South Atlantic Avenue. Turn left onto Dunlawton Avenue and continue for a total of 2 miles (3km) across Port Orange Bridge to South Nova Road (**SR 5A**). Turn right here and head north for ¼ mile (0.4km).*

Sugar Mill Gardens

13 The ruins of an old English sugar plantation here are of historical interest, but most people come for the 12-acre (5-hectare) botanical gardens. There are flowering trees, holly, magnolia and over 40 species of ivy. Children will enjoy four huge dinosaur statues—reminders of the gardens' former life as Bongoland.

Continue north for 2½ miles (4km), turn left onto South Street, then immediately right onto Museum Boulevard.

Daytona Museum of Arts and Sciences

14 The area's finest museum features two small but outstanding art collections—Arts in America, the best of paintings, furniture, metal,

Left: Fossil or sculpture? The Daytona Museum of Arts and Sciences will intrigue with its variety
Below: Ready to break records: year-round action for stock cars, race cars, motorcycles and go-karts at the Daytona International Speedway

glass and needlework from 1750 to 1917; and the Cuban Collection, two centuries of Latin folk art up to 1959, plus changing exhibits. The highlight of the prehistory gallery is a unique 13-foot (4m) skeleton of a giant ground sloth found nearby. There is a planetarium and also nature trails and sculpture gardens in the grounds.

*Return to South Nova Road and continue for 2 miles (3km) north to Volusia Avenue (**SR 600/US 92**). Turn left and head west.*

Daytona International Speedway

15 The World Center of Racing, opened in 1959, is possibly the most famous and most used racetrack in the world. On days when there are no events, the track is open to the public. You can ride in a small van on the apron of the banked curves and through the garage area on the 15- to 20-minute guided tour.

*Continue to **I-95**. Turn left, then right onto **I-4** for Orlando.*

BACKWOODS & SPRINGS

A fairy tale come true: mermaids put on a show in an underwater theater at Weeki Wachee Spring

ⓘ Orlando Visitor Information Center, Mercado Mediterranean Village, International Drive

*From Orlando head north on **I-4** to exit 33. Continue north on **US 17-92** to **US 441**. Turn off right onto **SR 436** and after 2½ miles (4km) turn left on Wekiwa Springs Road.*

Wekiwa Springs State Park

1 Wekiwa Springs is the headwater of the lush Wekiwa River, which flows into the St John's River. Activities here include swimming, canoe rental, 13 miles (21km) of hiking and nature trails and an 8-mile (13km) horseback-riding trail. The park is particularly good for bird-watching.

*Return to **US 441** and continue northwest for 11 miles (18km). Turn left following the signs to Mount Dora.*

Mount Dora

2 This delightful large village is closer in architectural character and atmosphere to New England than to central Florida and is a world away from the neon strips of Orlando. Tourists have been staying at the Lakeside Inn since 1883, its most famous guest being President Calvin Coolidge, who wintered here in 1930. The porch of this charming hotel is the perfect place to appreciate the village's lovely lakeside setting. The oldest and most picturesque building here, however, is the Victorian Gothic **Donnelly House**, built in 1882, and now a Masonic lodge (closed to the public). History buffs can visit the **Historical Society's Museum**, housed in the old jail (open in winter only) and browse the many antique shops in the quaint downtown district. Just southeast of Mount Dora is **Renninger's Antique Center**, which boasts 200 shops and claims the largest selection of antiques and collectibles in Florida (open Saturday and Sunday only).

ⓘ Mount Dora Chamber of Commerce, 341 North Alexander Street

*Continue through Mount Dora for some 6 miles (10km) to Tavares to rejoin **US 441**. After another 8 miles (13km) turn left on Canal Street following the signs for Leesburg.*

Venetian Gardens

3 Set on the reedy shores of Lake Harris, this lovely park garden is a perfect spot for a picnic. You will soon be joined by a host of ducks, assorted wading birds and squirrels.

*Rejoin **US 441** and head north for 21 miles (34km) to Belleview. Turn left onto **SR 484**.*

Don Garlits' Museum of Drag Racing

4 This is the world's only museum dedicated to those spectacular machines that tear along a ¼-mile

Orlando ● Wekiwa Springs State Park
Mount Dora ● Venetian Gardens
Don Garlits' Museum of Drag Racing ● Ocala
Appleton Museum of Art ● Silver Springs
Ocala National Forest ● Crystal River
Homosassa Springs ● Weeki Wachee Spring
Brooksville ● Clermont Citrus Tower ● Orlando

The futuristic fantasies of Orlando are left behind on this excursion into the heart of unspoiled north central Florida. From the 19th-century charm of Mount Dora, through the scenic Backwoods Trail and on into Ocala National Forest (where the world's largest sand pine forest survives), it seems time passes slowly in this neck of the woods. Silver Springs is one of central Florida's finest attractions and should be on the same must-see list as Universal Studios, Sea World and Cypress Gardens. However, the success of this attraction has inevitably brought some degree of commercialization, so if you are seeking a Florida without troops of fellow tourists, souvenir shops and the like, then you may like to try Juniper Springs. Water and more water seems to seep up everywhere through the limestone base in this part of Florida (Lake County alone boasts some 1,400 named lakes). You will see only a small fraction of these, but with an itinerary that includes Wekiwa Springs, Crystal River, Homosassa Springs and Weeki Wachee, take along your swimsuit and snorkel to get the maximum enjoyment from this trip.

SPECIAL TO . . .

5 *Ocala* Ocala is famous as the equine capital of the state, and around the town are some 400 horse farms. Many of these produce thoroughbreds, and counted on their roll of honor are no fewer than seven Kentucky Derby champions. Some farms are open to the public at specified times, offering tours and rides to suit all levels of experience. For an up-to-date list ask at the Chamber of Commerce.

FOR CHILDREN

7 *Silver Springs* Dinamation's **Dinosaurs Alive** at Silver Springs, the largest dinosaur exhibit in the southeastern United States, brilliantly re-creates these prehistoric monsters by means of sophisticated robotics. Some of the creatures can be controlled by levers, while others roar and lower frighteningly close—usually just as you are passing! (Note: admission charge is separate from Silver Springs.)

(0.4km) straight in under seven seconds. There are over 60 drag-racing cars dating from the earliest 1940s models and, for cognoscenti of the sport, these include cars belonging to Tom McEwen, Shirley Muldowney, Art Malone and of course 'Big Daddy' Don Garlits. Another 40 or so antique cars are on display, including one of the finest collections of early Fords anywhere.

*Return to **US 441** and head north for 11 miles (18km).*

Ocala

5 Sited on the western edge of Ocala National Forest, Ocala is a medium-sized regional center best known for nearby Silver Springs and for the area's thoroughbred horse farms. Just a short walk from the Chamber of Commerce is the **WMOP Museum of Sound**, which includes over a thousand radio sets, various Edison phonographs, music boxes and musical instruments (closed Sunday).

☐ Ocala Chamber of Commerce, 3rd Avenue

*Head northeast on **SR 40** for 4 miles (6km).*

Appleton Museum of Art

6 Inside this modern glistening marble building is probably the best fine art collection in central Florida. Among its 6,000 diverse objects are splendid primitive tribal masks and artifacts, exquisite Indian and Oriental treasures, antiquities from Asia, Africa and pre-Columbian South America and fine 19th-century paintings from Europe and America. All items are beautifully displayed. An elegant courtyard café provides light meals and snacks.

Continue east for 2 miles (3km).

Silver Springs

7 This multi-themed nature park enjoys one of the most beautiful settings in the state. At the heart of Silver Springs is the largest artesian limestone spring in the world, pumping an incredible 750 million US gallons (2.8 billion liters) of water each day. The highlight of the visit is a glass-bottom boat ride along the crystal-clear waters of the **Silver River** into a primeval, exotic, natural world of ancient cypress, moss-draped hundred-year-old oaks and tropical palms. Peer down and you will see many of the 36 different varieties of fish that swim here; look to the side and you will enjoy some 30 species of water birds, plus alligators and turtles. Blink and you will miss something! Luckily there is an equally fascinating glass-bottom ride along the **Lost River**, where you will also see a 1,200-year-old Timucuan Indian canoe, amazingly preserved under the waters. Aboard **Jungle Cruise** (the third boat ride), you will see several wild monkeys—a legacy of six of the original Tarzan movies that were filmed here—free-roaming giraffes, emus, gazelles and other non-native creatures. **Jeep Safari** is basically a land version of the boat cruises, visiting zebras, wild boars, many species of deer and birds, freely wandering through a natural wild habitat. In addition there is an excellent reptile show, bird and reptile displays, a petting zoo and an innovative new dinosaur display. The show and rides last 30 minutes each, so allow a full day here.

Adjacent to Silver Springs is **Wild Waters**. Designed more for the family than for dedicated water-

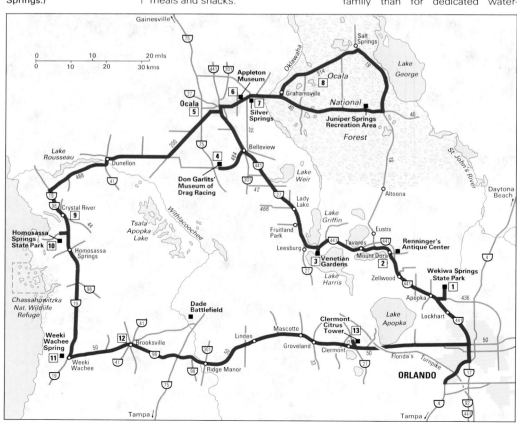

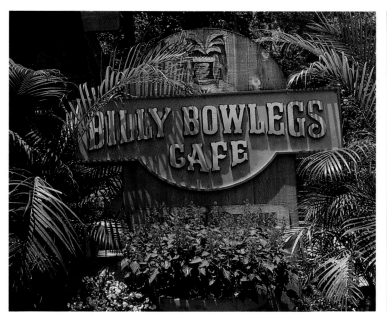

BACK TO NATURE

There are so many natural attractions on this route that it is hard to recommend an additional side trip. Some sites are more away from it all than others (for example, Juniper Springs is much less touristy than Silver Springs), but to get away altogether you may like to visit the **Chassahowitzka National Wildlife Refuge**. Home to bald eagles, manatees, turtles and peregrine falcons, the refuge is accessible only by boat, which can be rented from Chassahowitzka River Campground, just off **US 19**, 6 miles (10km) south of Homosassa Springs.

Above: Enjoy a taste of native hospitality when visiting the limpid waters of Silver Springs Right: The extraordinary clarity of the water at Silver Springs allows a superb view of underwater life

thrill seekers, it features seven water slides, flumes, a wave pool for body surfing, miniature golf and a volleyball area. The **Tad Pool** and a supervised water playground mean that you needn't worry about small children (closed during winter).

*Continue east on **SR 40** for 3 miles (5km).*

Ocala National Forest

8 The picturesque Oklawaha River is the eastern boundary of the forest. Turn left on SR 314. Continue west for 17 miles (27km) through the world's largest stand of sand pine. Turn right on **SR 19** and head south for 15 miles (24km) following the shore of Lake George, Florida's second largest lake. Turn right at **SR 40** and head west for 4 miles (6km) to **Juniper Springs Recreation Area**. The visitor center is housed in the picturesque old mill house, and the huge water wheel rolls over 8 million US gallons (30 million liters) of water per day.

For many people the highlight of Ocala National Forest is the 7-mile (11km) canoe trip from here, paddling peacefully through palm, cypress and live oak spotting birds, mammals, turtles and alligators. A shuttle service will bring you back to the recreation area.

*Continue west for 28 miles (45km) back to Ocala. Head southwest on **SR 200**, past several thoroughbred farms, for 14 miles (23km) and turn right on **SR 484** to Dunellon. Take **US 41** south for a short distance and turn right onto **SR 488**. After 12 miles (19km) turn left onto **US 19-98**. Head south for 6 miles (10km) and turn left onto **SR 44**.*

Crystal River

9 During the winter months manatees gather around the 72°F (22°C) crystal-clear spring-fed waters here. You can jump right in with them (wetsuit, snorkel and flippers are for rent) or just hire a boat and watch them. Glass-bottom trips also set out from here. Near by, the **Crystal River State Archaeological Site** marks

RECOMMENDED WALKS

Wekiwa Springs and Homosassa Springs both have fine nature trails. The Mount Dora Chamber of Commerce will also be happy to point out a historic walking trail to see this pretty town on foot.

SCENIC ROUTES

There are several scenic stretches on this route, most notably around Mount Dora, on **SR 200** (southwest of Ocala) and to the west of Ocala National Forest. The most scenic route from Mount Dora to Ocala is to head north on **SR 19** via Eustis, Umatilla and Altoona (the Backwoods Trail) into Ocala National Forest. Turn left onto **SR 40** to Juniper Springs and continue on the indicated route. (Note: this excludes Venetian Gardens and Don Garlits' Museum of Drag Racing.)

what is probably the longest continuously occupied site in Florida. For 1,600 years (between 200BC and AD1400) this was a ceremonial center where American Indians buried their dead and conducted trade.

*Return to **US 19** and head south for 3 miles (5km). Turn right on **SR 494** and continue for 1 mile (1.5km).*

Homosassa Springs State Park

10 If you can visit Crystal River only in the summer when the manatees are at sea, don't worry, because they congregate here all year round. You can see them, along with a multitude of fresh- and saltwater fish, in **The Spring of 10,000 Fish**, which you are taken to by boat. You then board a floating observatory, which allows you to go below the surface of the spring to enjoy an excellent vantage point. Displays along the park's nature trails include an extensive collection of wild birds. Just west of the park is the **Yulee Sugar Mill State Historic Site**. The mill, now a ruin, stood at the center of a 5,100-acre (2,062-hectare) sugar plantation, which was operated by around 1,000 slaves and supplied sugar products to Southern troops during the Civil War.

*Return to **US 19** and head south for 23 miles (37km).*

Weeki Wachee Spring

11 This is a spring with a difference, featuring an all-singing, all-dancing underwater mermaid show. The performers, taking lungfuls of air from submerged air lines, mime and act out the adventure of Hans Christian Andersen's *Little Mermaid* in the **Underwater Spring Theater**. Children love it, and adults are intrigued to see how it is done. The other highlight is the **Wilderness River Cruise**, where visitors can encounter Florida in its pristine unspoiled state (Weeki Wachee and Silver Springs share the same owners). An exotic bird show, a birds of prey show and a petting zoo containing farm animals complete a half-day's entertainment. Spend the rest of the day cooling off and have a picnic in adjacent **Buccaneer Bay**. This is Florida's only natural spring water park, with three water slides and a small beach (open March to September).

Weeki Wachee's water recreation area, Buccaneer Bay, with a beach, flume rides, a children's play area and picnic facilities

Feeding time for the manatees at Homosassa Springs. Fear not, the massive mammals are strict herbivores

*Head east on **SR 50** for 12 miles (19km).*

Brooksville

12 This large, attractive, sleepy village is home to a **Heritage Museum** (open Wednesday and Saturday) and **Roger's Christmas House Village**, with five themed houses that contain Christmas and gift items from around the world. Children delight in the Yuletide atmosphere, and grown-ups who are thinking ahead to next Christmas can take advantage of what is claimed to be the widest selection of ornaments in America. Just on the right as you leave Brooksville is the delightful **Blueberry Patch Tea Room**, a picture-book cornflower-blue country cottage furnished with antiques and serving fine food.

*Continue east on **US 98** for 13 miles (21km) before picking up eastbound **SR 50**. Continue for a further 29 miles (47km), then turn left onto **US 27** and head north for 1 mile (1.5km).*

Clermont Citrus Tower

13 This towering landmark, which measures 226 feet (69m) high, is 543 feet (166m) above sea level, giving it the honor of being Florida's highest point. The tower was built to provide an observation deck so that tourists could enjoy the sight of the citrus groves stretching out over the rolling hills below. Unfortunately, the freezes of recent years have decimated the crop, and although many groves have been replanted, there are few orange trees in view at present.

Adjacent to the tower is the **House of Presidents Wax Museum** where you can meet all the US presidents from Washington to Bush.

*Return south to **US 50** and continue east to return to Orlando (**I-4** exit 41).*

FOR HISTORY BUFFS

12 *Brooksville* 'Have a good heart; our difficulties and dangers are over now, and as soon as we arrive at Fort King you will have three days to rest and keep Christmas gaily.' This was the last address that Major Francis Dade made to his command of 108 cold, tired men at this site on December 28, 1835. Within eight hours all but three were dead, victims of an ambush that marked the beginning of the Second Seminole Indian War. The inglorious story of this bloody chapter in Florida's history is told in the visitor center at Dade Battlefield State Historic Park. There is also an interpretive trail. The site is open Thursday to Monday and is located northeast of Brooksville.

2/3 days — 203 miles (327km)

KISSIMMEE & CYPRESS GARDENS

**Orlando ● Winter Haven ● Cypress Gardens
Bok Tower Gardens ● Lake Wales
Lake Kissimmee State Park
Tupperware Convention Center
Flying Tigers Warbirds Museum ● Old Town
Water Mania ● Orlando**

On the very doorstep of Walt Disney World, Kissimmee (pronounced Kiss-SIM-me) appears to be just a dormitory town of economy hotels and budget family attractions. Head south and you will find Cypress Gardens, another of Florida's famous theme parks. This one, however, is quiet and mostly natural, far removed from the hustle and bustle of Mickey's world. Keep heading south on this route and the tourist veneer becomes even thinner until you finally get to Yeehaw Junction. Little more than a signpost on the roadside, this gloriously named spot marks Cracker Country, the old Florida of wide-open spaces and cattle-ranches. As you cruise along US 192 with its bright lights, it seems hardly likely that Kissimmee is still a major cattle-ranching center, but just a few miles away its rich hinterland unfurls.

⏽ Orlando Visitor Information Center, Mercado Mediterranean Village, International Drive

From Orlando head south on I-4 for 27 miles (43km) to exit 22. Turn left onto SR 557 and head south for Winter Haven.

Traditional Southern Belles grace the grounds of Cypress Gardens, a paradise on earth for flower lovers

Winter Haven

1 There is not a great deal to see here, but sports fans may like to know that this small town is indeed the winter haven for the Boston Red Sox baseball team from late February to early April. You can see them training at **Chain O'Lakes Park** (on Cypress Gardens Boulevard). Close by, **Baseball City**, at the junction of **US 27** and **I-4**, is the home of the Baseball City Royals, a class A team in the Florida state league. With so much water hereabouts, fishing is also very popular, and the Southeast's largest **fishing museum** (closed weekends) is located at the intersection of Recker Road (**SR 655**) and Spirit Lake Road.

⏽ Winter Haven Chamber of Commerce, 401 Avenue B, NW (one block east of **US 17**)

*Turn left onto Cypress Gardens Boulevard (**SR 540**), 3 miles (5km).*

Cypress Gardens

2 This is Florida's longest-established theme park, though by today's standards it is hardly recognizable as such. Yet what it lacks in technological wizardry and thrill rides, it more than makes up for in natural beauty and some of the state's most athletic performers. Chief among these is **The Greatest American Ski Show**, which features many of the best water skiers in the country. Barefooting, kite-flying and the formation of amazing human pyramids are just some of their specialties. **Air Dancin'** is an acrobatics extravaganza, and **Classical Ice** is an outstanding ice-skating revue complete with lasers and dancing waters. The park's Deep South theme is personified by the famous Southern Belles, who pose pretty as a picture, in their hooped antebellum skirts, among the beautifully manicured gardens. With around 8,000 varieties of exotic plants and flowers, it is no wonder that *Life* magazine described Cypress Gardens as 'a photographer's paradise'.

For the best overview of the grounds jump aboard the **Kodak Island in the Sky**, a revolving platform on a crane-like arm, which hauls its way up from ground level to 153 feet (47m) high.

To observe things at closer quarters, take the **Botanical Gardens Cruise**, preferably early in the morning to avoid waiting in line. Around the old-time **Southern Crossroads**, where banjo players and barbershop quartets entertain, are exotic animal habitats, a huge free-flight aviary, a tropical bird show, an entertaining reptile-handling demonstration and one of the country's most elaborate model railroads. Allow for nearly a full day here.

*Follow **SR 540** east crossing **US 27** to **US 27 (Alt)** and turn right (south). Turn left onto **SR 17A**, 8 miles (13 km).*

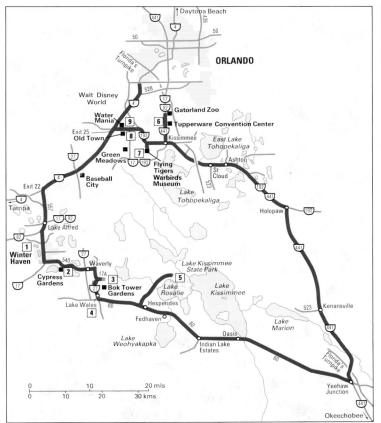

Bok Tower Gardens

3 Bok Tower is located on the Florida peninsula's highest point, **Iron Mountain**, with an elevation of 295 feet (90m). The bell tower, which is the visual centerpiece of these beautiful gardens, is made up of colored marble from Georgia, set off with brass, iron and ceramic friezes recalling the plant and animal motifs of Persia and India and images from Greece and China. Bearing Gothic and Art Deco influences, it was built between 1927 and 1928. Standing 205 feet (62m) high, it houses 57 bronze bells varying in weight from 17 pounds (7.7kg) to almost 12 US tons (10.8 metric tons). You can hear recitals daily at 3pm. The tower has never been open to the public, but an

A spectacular water-ski revue is performed by top American skiers at Cypress Gardens

FOR HISTORY BUFFS

3 *Bok Tower Gardens* A 'new' old feature opened at Bok Gardens to celebrate the 1992 Columbian Quincentennial is **Pinewood House and Garden**. This eagerly awaited restoration has unveiled one of the finest examples of Mediterranean Revival landscape and residential design, including furnishings, in the whole state. Admission is by tours only (lasting 50 minutes), which run from mid-September to mid-May on Tuesdays, Thursdays and Sundays. Register at the information booth.

BACK TO NATURE

3 *Bok Tower Gardens* From Bok Tower Gardens' **Window by the Pond nature observatory**, the lucky visitor might see belted kingfishers, purple gallinules, egrets and herons fishing a few feet away from the picture window. **Green Meadows Children's Farm** educates people of all ages as to what goes on down on the farm, and a 2-hour guided tour gets you right up close to pigs, cows, goats, sheep, turkeys, ducks and other resident animals.

SCENIC ROUTES

The lake area around Winter Haven provides for pleasant driving, and **US 27 (Alt)** south to Lake Wales is officially designated as a scenic route, though in fact there is not much to see. The area from Yeehaw Junction to Holopaw is regarded as old Cracker farming Florida, and here you will see great stretches of fields and cattle pasture.

FOR CHILDREN

The Kissimmee area is bursting with children's attractions. In addition to those on the itinerary, older children may enjoy **Reptile World Serpentarium** (on **East US 192** towards St Cloud), an educational indoor display and scientific venom-production facility. Younger ones will love a hands-on day at **Green Meadows Children's Farm** (5 miles/8km south on Poinciana Boulevard), and all ages can have fun on the go-karts and fairground rides at **Fun 'n' Wheels** (close to Osceola Square Mall).

RECOMMENDED WALKS

The most peaceful place for a walk is either at **Bok Tower Gardens** for a leisurely stroll or at **Lake Kissimmee State Park** for a more serious hike. At the former the North Walk is lined with many seasonal blossoming plants, including giant crinum with enormous lily-like flowers, while the rougher Pine Ridge Trail traverses the original vegetation of Iron Mountain. At the state park there are 13 miles (21km) of prairie and woodland hiking routes to choose from.

audiovisual program in the visitors center shows its inner machinery. The garden is one of Florida's most peaceful places. Azaleas, camellias, magnolias, gardenias and other flowering shrubs provide magnificent colors against dark green ferns, palms, oaks and pines. The grounds are also home to several species of wading birds.

Return to US 27 (Alt) and continue south for 1¼ miles (2km). At the traffic lights turn left onto North Avenue (SR 17A) and left onto Spook Hill.

Lake Wales

4 Spook Hill is certainly the most curious of this small town's attractions, though in Florida a steep hill of any kind is a curiosity in itself. Park on the white line facing up the steep side of the hill, release your brake and you apparently roll up the hill (don't expect to roll forwards up the really steep part of the hill—that really would be impossible!). An optical illusion? An Indian curse? Find out more at the Chamber of Commerce.

Spook Hill is a one-way street, so head back in a circle to the traffic lights and then continue a short distance to **The Depot**, a restored railroad building which serves as the **Lake Wales Museum and Cultural Center**. Naturally enough, this houses train memorabilia and a turn-of-the-century Pullman car. You can also learn about local cattle ranching and citrus farming.

🛈 Lake Wales Chamber of Commerce, Central Avenue

Continue south on US 27 (Alt) and turn left to the junction with SR 60. Drive east to pick up Boy Scout Road heading north, then follow the signs on Camp Mack Road to Lake Kissimmee (15 miles/24km east of Lake Wales).

Lake Kissimmee State Park

5 The park comprises 5,000 acres (2,024 hectares) bordering three lakes, and among its floodplain prairies, marshes and pine flatwoods roam white-tailed deer, bald eagles, sandhill cranes and wild turkey. An observation platform provides a fine view over Lake Kissimmee, while canoes are available for a closer look at the park's waterways. The best time to visit is at the weekend when the park features a living-history 1876 **Cow Camp**. This was (and still is) cowboy country, and you can see one of the few remaining herds of scrub cattle still in existence. A cow camp consists of a holding pen where the cows are branded and a crude shelter for the cow hunters (as they call themselves), so don't expect to see a re-creation of Dodge City.

Return to SR 60 and continue east for 37 miles (60km) to Yeehaw Junction. Turn left and head north on US 441 for 35 miles (56km). Turn left at Holopaw onto US 192-441 and follow this northwest for 24 miles (39km). Turn right onto the South Orange Blossom Trail (US 441/ 17-92), 107 miles (172km).

Tupperware Convention Center

6 The Tupperware Convention Center is certainly an unusual attraction, and considering that it is not even a factory tour, its popularity is even more surprising. However, if you would like to learn about the history of food containers from Egyptian times to today's ubiquitous Tupperware container, you will be made very welcome and it is free. Close by, at **Gatorland Zoo**, boardwalks cross the habitat of over

Gatorland Zoo specializes in 'gators, crocs, snakes and other reptiles. Not for the squeamish

5,000 alligators, ranging in length from a few inches to 15 feet (4.6m). Watch them leap out of the water at feeding time in the Gator Jumparoo Show. The alligator feeding frenzy scenes for *Indiana Jones and the Temple of Doom* were filmed here.

*Return south to **US 192** (West Irlo Bronson Memorial Highway) and turn right.*

Flying Tigers Warbirds Museum

7 Along with International Drive, Kissimmee is the most important accommodation area for Disney visitors, and there is no shortage of attractions along this strip. If you have not experienced an airboat ride or would like to pilot your own, stop at U-Drive Airboat Rentals for a look beyond the neon in Kissimmee.

To the left off **SR 531**, toward Kissimmee Airport, the Flying Tigers Warbirds Air Museum, featuring a Mustang, a Flying Fortress, a Tiger Moth and several World War II survivors. Back on **US 192** you can enjoy a four-course dinner and watch jousting knights rescue damsels in distress at **Medieval Times** (reservations recommended). This popular dinner attraction has also spawned a daytime museum-village with craft workshops, birds of prey, and a dungeon and torture chamber. There are two other themed dinner stops on this strip: **Fort Liberty**, a rowdy Western-style evening with ranch chow, and **Arabian Nights**, featuring a cast of some 60 horses and a chariot race. For an encounter with real cow hunters, however, head for Kissimmee's most authentic attraction—its weekly cattle auction, held every Wednesday from 8am to around noon at the market on East Donegan Avenue (just north of **US 17-92** and **US 441**). After the auction folks congregate at the improbably named **Osceola Q Coach Woodruff's Rib Cage** market restaurant for some of the best barbecued beef this side of the Rockies.

ℹ️ Kissimmee/St Cloud Convention and Visitors Bureau, US 192 East

*Further west on **US 192** is Old Town.*

Old Town

8 Kissimmee's answer to Orlando's Church Street is the focus for tourist nightlife. **Little Darlin's Rock 'n' Roll Palace** is the mainstay and often features live rock legends from the '50s and '60s. Otherwise Old Town resembles Disney's Main Street USA, with some 70 shops and restaurants harking back to turn-of-the-century America. For Elvis Presley fans the high point is the largest collection of memorabilia relating to The King outside Gracelands, including costumes, limosines and guns (a smaller collection is on International Drive, Orlando).

By comparison, the 'Wonderful wooden trains of Walter T Potter' (housed in the **Great Train Store and Exhibit**) may seem tame, but this beautifully crafted collection is well worth a look. If you are not a rock 'n' roll fan, it may well be the highlight of Old Town.

In Kissimmee, the next best thing to Gracelands for fans of Elvis

Almost opposite Old Town is Water Mania.

Water Mania

9 This is the smallest of the water parks in the Orlando area, but it still offers plenty of thrills and relaxation. It boasts the 72-foot (22m) **Screamer**, and family rides such as the **Anaconda**, where a four-person raft twists and turns through 400 feet (122m), and the **Banana Peel**, a two-person water-chute plunge. There is also the second biggest wave pool in Florida, with eight different wave patterns, and the **Double Beserker**, where two people race each other to the bottom in directly adjacent slides. A sand beach, a shady picnic area, a maze and other dry amusements complete a lazy day's entertainment (closed December through February).

*Rejoin **I-4** (exit 25) and return north to Orlando, 23 miles (37km).*

Orlando–Winter Haven **30 (48)**
Winter Haven–Cypress Gardens **3 (5)**
Cypress Gardens–Bok Tower
Gardens **8 (13)**
Bok Tower Gardens–Lake Wales **3 (5)**
Lake Wales–Lake Kissimmee State
Park **15 (24)**
Lake Kissimmee State Park–
Tupperware Convention Center **107
(172)**
Tupperware Convention Center–Flying
Tigers **8 (13)**
Flying Tigers–Old Town **6 (10)**
Old Town–Water Mania **0 (0)**
Water Mania–Orlando **23 (37)**

SPECIAL TO . . .

The **Silver Spurs Rodeo** is held every February and July at the Silver Spurs Arena in Kissimmee. This features some of the South's top professional cowboys competing for a fistful of dollars in events such as calf roping, steer wrestling, saddle and bareback riding. Spectators are also treated to live country music and the Silver Spurs Quadrille Team, which performs its brand of square dancing on horseback.

THE FIRST COAST

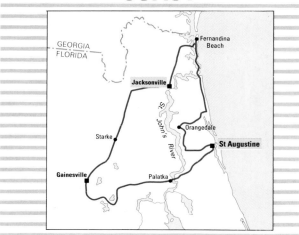

Florida saw the arrival of its first Europeans on Easter morning in 1513, when Juan Ponce de León landed near the site of St Augustine. Claiming the land for Spain, he named it after the Spanish Feast of Flowers at Easter, Pascua Florida. León did not stay, however, and it was left to his fellow countryman, Pedro Menéndez de Avilés, to return in 1565 to found the first European settlement at St Augustine. The French followed hard on the Spaniard's heels, but rued their ambitions later that year when Menéndez wiped out their settlement and its inhabitants. Spain's other great contemporary rival, England, also had designs on the strategically important First Coast harbors, and in 1585 Sir Francis Drake burned St Augustine to the ground. It was not until 1763, however, that the British took Florida, and then it was a bloodless victory: the Spaniards handed over this territory peacefully in order to regain recently captured Havana.

Twenty years later it was the turn of the British to horse-trade territories, and the First Coast (and Florida) reverted to Spanish rule. Of course, the territorial period of Florida's history was not restricted just to the northeast, but nowhere was it more dramatic than here and, arguably, nowhere in the whole US is it better interpreted for the visitor than here.

The highlight is the beautiful, European-style old-world town of St Augustine. Although for some it has become a little too cocooned within its rich history, the tiny streets and alleyways and its charming lodgings are a breath of fresh air after the characterless malls and resort hotels found elsewhere in the state. Just north of Jacksonville, the pretty Victorian gingerbread mansions and shops of Amelia Island continue the history lesson, moving through the late 19th and early 20th century.

During the late 19th century, millionaire developer Henry Flagler started his East Coast ambitions at St Augustine by building three of his finest hotels. In terms of a lasting effect on tourism, however, the Flagler influence is much less marked here than further south. Significantly, none of Flagler's St Augustine hotels are still open as hotels. In hindsight this would seem to have been fortuitous for the First Coast, as the region retains a sense of history and a quiet charm far removed from the brash resorts of the southeast.

City Tour 8

St Augustine, where it all began, is the most sensible starting point for a tour of the First Coast. It is also worth stressing that despite its deep historical roots, it is also the most complete all-round resort town in northeast Florida. A walking tour of the old city will tell you all you want to know about the colonial period, but don't try to do it all in one day. There is far too much to see, and you will soon overdose on 'oldest' buildings, stores and 'oldest' claims of all kinds. The beach and its family attractions are a perfect antidote.

Tour 14

The Jacksonville beaches are every bit as good as their more famous rivals to the south, and visitors with a sense of history will appreciate the old ports, the even older forts and Florida's oldest plantation. The charming northeastern-most town of Fernandina Beach is arguably as rich in history and architecture as the state's southernmost point, Key West. It is an excellent all-round resort, and

its relative lack of fame only adds to the enjoyment of those who are in the know.

Gainesville is another understated town which will reward the curious visitor. Here there are no skyscrapers, just elegant red-brick University of Florida buildings, an historic district and some fine outdoor attractions. Drive a little further south and it seems time has stood still. Paynes Prairie is almost primeval and the village of Micanopy seems locked in an 1800s time capsule. It is not hard to see why novelist Marjorie Kinnan Rawlings loved Cross Creek so dearly. It, too, harkens back to a peaceful, almost disappeared, Florida.

City Tour 9

Thanks to some imaginative developments and first-rate visitor attractions, the city of Jacksonville is currently enjoying an upswing in its tourism fortunes. With its glittering skyscrapers and new waterside developments, it is like a smaller version of Miami, and city slickers are bound to enjoy it.

Authentically costumed volunteers provide a more palatable dimension to St Augustine's restored Spanish Quarter

Futuristic towers rise as modern statements of architecture on the Jacksonville skyline

ST AUGUSTINE

St Augustine Visitor Center ● The Oldest Drug Store
The Oldest Wooden Schoolhouse
Spanish Quarter ● Plaza de la Constitución
The Oldest Store Museum ● Ximenez-Fatio House
González-Alvarez House ● Lightner Museum
Flagler College ● Castillo de San Marcos
Ripley's Believe It or Not!
Mission of Nombre de Dios ● Fountain of Youth
The Old Jail ● Alligator Farm ● Fort Matanzas
Marineland of Florida
Washington Oaks State Gardens ● St Augustine

St Augustine, founded in 1565, is the oldest permanent European settlement in the continental United States. A walk down St George Street is like stepping back in time over two centuries and more. This beautiful, narrow, flower-decked street, with its overhanging wooden balconies, is at its best at any festival time, when it seems that every other person is in period costume. History here is living, vibrant and interpreted with enthusiasm and a smile. The Flagler hotels from Florida's Gilded Age provide a historical break from colonial days, and when you want to escape from the past altogether, St Augustine Beach is a fine resort in its own right. The superlatives continue, however, with the oldest marine-life park and the oldest alligator zoo.

RECOMMENDED WALKS

Those who still have the energy after walking around the old city can escape from the crowds at Washington Oaks State Gardens. Take a walk through the ornamental gardens, with their towering live oaks, out along the river and on to the dramatic rocky shore.

Park just outside the old city boundaries. Walk through the parking lot past the early 19th-century Huguenot Cemetery and enter the old city through the stone gateposts. Turn immediately right onto Orange Street.

Oldest Drug Store

1 This ancient-looking cypress-boarded building was originally built in 1739 to sell liquor, medicine and Indian remedies. It has been a pharmacy ever since 1887 and it now houses a fine display of memorabilia from its early days, up to the 1950s,

Period attire equips this lady for celebrating one of St Augustine's ubiquitous festivals

with many original shopfittings. Visitors are greeted by the 'shop-keeper' himself, who may well classify as 'the oldest animatronic' (Disney-style robot). Just behind the store on Cordova Street is the **Museum Theater**, which presents an opportunity to see the history of St Augustine on film.

Return to the old city gate and follow St George Street.

The Oldest Wooden Schoolhouse

2 Another atmospheric red cedar and cypress-boarded building, this structure is held together by wooden pegs and hand-made nails. It was built some time before 1763 and is thought to be the country's oldest schoolhouse. You can see a 'class' in session and the spartan upstairs accommodation where the school-master lived. The kitchen building to the rear is set in a charming garden.

Continue down St George Street.

Spanish Quarter (San Augustin Antiguo)

3 The centerpiece of the old city, this superb living history village depicts everyday colonial life in the mid-18th century. You can visit a Minorcan family house, a foot soldier's dwelling (incorporating a store), an officer's house, a blacksmith's shop, a spinning and weaving area and other houses. The enthusiastic costumed guides and craftspeople use only period tools and materials as part of their faithful re-creation of the past.

Continue along St George Street to the end of the pedestrians-only section.

Plaza de la Constitución

4 This was the business district during the Spanish heyday and across the square to the left stands a statue of Ponce de León, who claimed Florida for Spain in 1513. Immediately left is the handsome basilica **Cathedral of St Augustine**, built in 1797, though considerably reconstructed inside. Across the square is the rather uninspired **Potter's Wax Museum** and adjacent is the **Lyons Maritime Museum** which claims the largest collection of deep-sea diving helmets in the world. Just off the plaza on Avilés Street (by the Maritime Museum) is the **Spanish Military Hospital**, which is an outlying part of the Spanish Quarter. This is also well worth a visit to see its apothecary and wards, presented as they were in 1791.

Continue along Avilés Street and turn right onto Artillery Street.

The Oldest Store Museum

5 This authentic turn-of-the-century general store is crammed full with over 100,000 nostalgic items evoking the days of high, stiff clip-on collars, lace-up corsets and Edison phonographs. It also holds a small **museum** of antique vehicles, high-

wheeled bicycles and farm artifacts.

Return to and continue along Avilés Street.

Ximenez-Fatio House

6 This beautiful historic house operated as a fashionable inn from 1855 to 1875. Its furnishings reflect this period, and a guided tour will point out the English and Spanish design features. From the balcony you can look across to the 1763 **Casa de Solana**, which serves today's tourists bed and breakfast, and see how little has changed in old St Augustine.

Turn left on Bridge Street, right on Charlotte Street and left on St Francis Street.

The time-wearied façade of González-Alvarez, the oldest house in America

González-Alvarez House

7 This site has been continuously occupied since the early 1600s, and the present house is thought to date from the first decade of the 18th century. It reflects the simple lifestyle of the earliest Spanish settlers, the subsequent British influences, and the territorial American changes and additions. On the same site is a general **history museum**, a **Museum of Florida's Army**, and

Over 100,000 curios from original stock evoke turn-of-the-century life at the Oldest Store Museum

SCENIC ROUTES

The coast drive south along **SR A1A** to Washington Oaks State Gardens is an officially designated scenic route, but for a really picturesque water vista take a cruise on board one of the *Victory* cruisers, or the beautiful wooden sailing vessel *Camelot*, all of which depart from the City Yacht Pier, adjacent to the Bridge of Lions. The bridge and Matanzas Bay are particularly pretty by night, and by day you can see oyster beds, salt marshes, and perhaps leaping dolphins.

BACK TO NATURE

Anastasia State Recreation Area at St Augustine Beach is excellent for bird-watching. Sandpipers, gulls, terns and pelicans are common along the shore, while herons and egrets frequent the lagoon and marshes. Fifteen miles (24km) south of St Augustine, **Faver-Dykes State Park** is a haven of peace and quiet. Canoe along the creek, and among the pine flatwoods and hammock you might see deer, wild turkeys, hawks and bobcats.

FOR HISTORY BUFFS

Needless to say, the whole area is a paradise for history lovers. González-Alvarez House (the Oldest House), the Spanish Quarter and the Fountain of Youth are the bare essentials, but to get away from the crowds visit Flagler College, then pay your respects to Florida's greatest pioneer at the beautiful Memorial Presbyterian Church on Sevilla Street, behind the college. Designed in 1889 by Flagler in Venetian Renaissance style as a memorial to his daughter, this is also his last resting place.

Oriental elegance on a palatial scale befits Flagler College's past life as a hotel for the rich

lovely ornamental gardens, which contain plants typical of those grown by the occupants of the house.

Walk back up St Francis Street, turn right past the 1791 St Francis Inn onto St George Street. Follow it to the Plaza de la Constitución and turn left onto King Street.

Lightner Museum

8 The stately Spanish Renaissance-style edifice in which the Lightner Museum resides was built by Henry Flagler in 1888 as the Alcazar Hotel. Monied guests once stayed in what now exhibits an outstanding collection of Victorian American and European art, antiques and furnishings, Oriental pieces, mechanical musical instruments (played once a day) and a sparkling display of American Brilliant Period cut crystal and Tiffany glass. Signs and photographs tell the story of the hotel, and the steam baths can still be seen *in situ*. Below the museum collection the former swimming pool now houses the **Lightner Antique Shopping Mall** and an elegant café-restaurant. Adjacent to the museum is **Zorayda Castle**, an architectural reproduction of the Moorish Alhambra Palace in Granada, Spain. Its artifacts are not without interest, but there is a disappointing lack of authentic atmosphere, hardly helped by American piped music. Next door is a **Museum of Weapons and Early American History**.

Cross the road opposite the Lightner to Flagler College.

Flagler College

9 The Alcazar's sister hotel was the equally magnificent Ponce de León. The hotel closed its doors in 1967 and since 1971 has been home to the highly regarded liberal arts Flagler College. A guided tour of the marble lobby area, the gracious grand parlor and elegant dining hall allows you to see more of the trappings of Florida's Gilded Age. A third Flagler hotel on the same square, the Cordova (born as the Casa Monica), now functions as the **City Hall complex**.

Follow Cordova Street north, past Victorian bed and breakfast inns, as far as Orange Street. Turn right to get back to the old city gate. Follow San Marco Avenue to the castle entrance.

Castillo de San Marcos

10 Built between 1672 and 1695 to guard homeward-bound Spanish galleons against corsairs, this is the oldest stone fort in America. During its 300 years of constant active service it has played host to the British, during the American Revolution, to the unwilling Chief Osceola and his Seminole tribe, held captive here in 1835, and to troops from both the North and the South during the Civil War. The huge imposing walls made from coquina (a natural shellstone) measure some 33 feet (10m) high and are up to 14 feet (4.3m) thick at the base. Now a national monument, its rangers will provide you with an introductory history, then let you explore its rooms, exhibits and battlements.

Return to the parking lot at the information center. Opposite is Ripley's Believe It or Not!

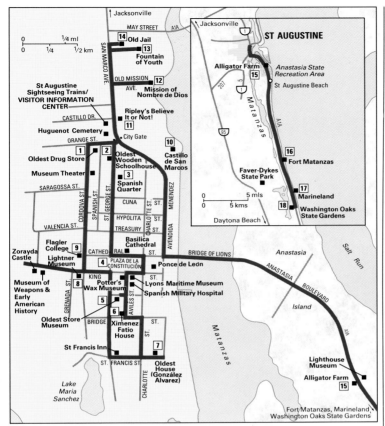

FOR CHILDREN

Most youngsters will enjoy seeing the conditions their peers lived under some two centuries ago at the Oldest Wooden Schoolhouse, and a swing on the noisy school bell in the garden is irresistible. For a break from the city's history lessons, however, children (of all ages) will love the funhouse style and unexpected tricks of Ripley's Believe It or Not! Museum, as well as marveling at its exhibits. On the beach side of town, Alligator Farm and Marineland are guaranteed child-pleasers.

Ripley's Believe It or Not!

11 Robert Ripley, the self-billed 'modern Marco Polo', traveled to 198 countries during the early part of this century, and whenever he saw an oddity he collected it. This museum features some 750 objects from his extraordinary treasure trove, and whether or not trivia, record-breakers and freaks appeal to you, there is never a dull moment here. Marvel at how the Mona Lisa was created from 63 slices of toasted bread, gasp at the 24-foot (7.3m) Eiffel Tower made up of 110,000 toothpicks, and shudder at the real shrunken human heads! The final 'believe it or not' is that **Castle Warden**, the grand building in which the museum is housed, was once home to the great American novelist Marjorie Kinnan Rawlings, of Cross Creek fame (see Gainesville Tour 14).

Follow San Marco Avenue five blocks north to Old Mission Avenue and turn right.

Mission of Nombre de Dios

12 One of the most sacred and historic places in the country, the mission stands on the site where, in 1565, Pedro Menéndez de Avilés, admiral of the Spanish fleet, stepped ashore and the first Mass in America was celebrated. The place was called Nombre de Dios (Name of God), and a mission and the first Marian shrine, Nuestra Señora de la Leche, were established. A stainless steel cross towering 208 feet (63m) high marks the site of the founding of St Augustine.

Return to San Marco Avenue, continue north for three blocks and turn right.

Would you dare to annoy this formidable exhibit at Ripley's Believe It or Not!?

Fountain of Youth

13 Predating the mission by 52 years in the history of European discovery is the Fountain of Youth site. This is the spot where it is thought Ponce de León first set foot on Florida soil in 1513, possibly searching for the fabled Fountain of Youth as well as for gold. An ancient spring does, in fact, still flow here, and visitors are given a free taste. The surrounding **archaeological park** also contains a planetarium, an audiovisual display showing how León navigated by the stars, excavations of a 2,000-year-old Timucuan Indian settlement, and the first Christian Indian burial ground in North America.

Return to San Marco Avenue, continue north one block and turn right.

The Old Jail

14 This grim edifice, built in 1890, served as the St John's County Jail until 1953. The jokey courtyard displays of felons in black and white hooped prison suits contrast with the forbidding crumbling cell block and the collection of weapons taken away from incarcerated criminals.

*Return south on San Marco Avenue, collect your car, and cross the Bridge of Lions (so named after its stone beasts). Continue on **SR A1A** for 2 miles (3km).*

Festivals and Spanish fiestas are a way of life here. Try to catch **Days in Spain** at the end of August or the **Cross & Sword** dramatic musical pageantry (Florida's state play), staged every night from mid-June through late August (except Sundays). The **Spanish Night Watch** and the **British Night Watch** (third Saturday in June and first Saturday in December respectively) see torchlight processions to the Castillo, and on 15 February the birth of the city's founder, Pedro Menéndez, is celebrated.

Alligator Farm

15 Established in 1893, this is the world's original alligator attraction. In addition to its hundreds of scaly residents, you can see the Snappin' Sam Show, the **Mystic Alligator Swamp** and the **Florida Wildlife Show**. An elevated board-walk winds through a beautiful lagoon, and in late afternoon flocks of heron, egret and ibis return here to roost. Ironically the star of the farm is a huge crocodile, Gomek from New Guinea, said to be the largest captive reptile in the Western hemisphere.

Opposite the farm is the **Light-house Museum**. This landmark was built between 1871 and 1876. It now houses a coastal and maritime museum and a gallery featuring local artists. Climb to the top for a fine view of town and bay.

*Continue south, to the resort of St Augustine Beach (information center on **SR A1A**) and on for a further 9 miles (14km).*

Fort Matanzas

16 Matanzas, Spanish for slaughter, refers to the attack at this site in 1565 in which 200 to 300 unarmed French Huguenots were put to the sword by the Spanish Catholic forces of Menéndez to counter French territorial encroachment and their perceived religious heresy. The well-preserved fort was built of coquina between 1740 and 1742 by Menéndez's successors to prevent any approach to St Augustine along the Intracoastal Waterway.

Human nature's appetite for the macabre has financed Alligator Farm since 1893

Continue south for 4 miles (6km).

Marineland of Florida

17 This fine marine-life park, claimed to be the oldest in the world, has been delighting audiences for over 50 years without losing any of its orig-inality or sparkle. You may well have seen leaping dolphins and barking sea lions before, but Marineland does it so well it is worth seeing again. Exceptional, too, is the underwater hand-feeding of sharks, barracuda and stingrays, and performing electric eels. *Sea Dream* is a 3-D movie where monsters of the deep seem to come right out of the screen, **Wonders of the Spring** is one of the country's largest freshwater aquariums, stocked with every type of Florida freshwater fish, and during the sum-mer 'The Great American High Dive' goes down well with everyone.

Continue south for 3 miles (5km).

Washington Oaks State Gardens

18 In contrast to the flat shores of St Augustine Beach, the ocean waves here have washed away the sand to create a picturesque boulder-strewn beach. Bird-watchers should arrive at low tide. Designated by the state parks system as an under-utilized 'gem', the gardens are a fine place for a picnic.

*Return to St Augustine north on **SR A1A**.*

Ladder 7 of the St Augustine Fire Department. Twentieth-century architecture dictates the magnitude of modern firefighting equipment

JACKSONVILLE BEACH

*From St Augustine follow **SR 214** west 14 miles (23km) to Tocoi on the St John's River. Follow the river north on **SR 13** for a further 17 miles (27km) to Orangedale. Turn right onto **SR 210** and follow it northeast to the coast where it joins **SR A1A**. Turn north for Jacksonville Beach. (For a more direct, though less scenic route, simply take **SR A1A** north from St Augustine for 29 miles (47km).)*

St Augustine ● Jacksonville Beach ● Mayport
Kingsley Plantation ● Little Talbot Island
Amelia Island ● Fernandina Beach
Jacksonville City Tour ● Gainesville
Paynes Prairie State Preserve ● Cross Creek
Ravine State Gardens, Palatka ● St Augustine

Jacksonville Beach

1 This is the centerpiece and liveliest of the four Jacksonville beaches, which stretch for some 7 miles (11km) as far as Ponte Vedra Beach (south of this are more fine beaches, some of which are totally undeveloped). Just off the beach at North First Street is the **Beaches Art and Craft Gallery**, a cooperative showroom featuring the works of some 40 local artists. Seawalk Plaza also regularly has art exhibits and festivals. On Beach Boulevard is the **Beaches Antique Gallery**, north Florida's largest antique mall with over 120 dealers, and **Pablo Historical Park and Old House Museum**. Here you can see turn-of-the-century railroad memorabilia, including a 31-US-ton (28,500kg) locomotive and the stationmaster's home, and a costumed guide will entertain you with tales of what life was life in the Old House back in the 1900s. History buffs may also enjoy the American **Lighthouse Museum** at North Third Street. The adjacent beaches of Neptune and Atlantic are quieter and good for surfing. The area's best beach is at **Kathryn Abbey Hanna Park**, north of Atlantic, with 1½ miles (2km) of lovely white sand and scenic nature trails.

*Continue north on **SR A1A**.*

In honor of its historical importance and also because it sits at the top of the state, the northeastern tip of Florida is sometimes called The Crown. Certainly the city of Jacksonville is one of Florida's most valuable jewels, and the golden Jacksonville beaches, as lively or as nearly deserted as you wish, are an excellent family vacation choice. The nickname of this coast, the Buccaneer Trail, is indicative of the wealth of history here and commemorates such villains and heroes (depending on your allegiances) as Jean Lafitte, Blackbeard and Sir Francis Drake. Fittingly, the jewel in the Crown is the lovingly restored Fernandina Beach, at the northernmost tip of the state. Almost hidden to the south is Alachua County, where life goes on as it has for centuries, undisturbed by tourism. Surprisingly, however, there is still plenty for the visitor to see and experience. Gainesville is a solid all-American university town with some unusual natural attractions, while its country hinterland inspired Marjorie Kinnan Rawlings to write some of America's best-loved literature. Visitors looking for a piece of the real, unadulterated Florida will probably be inspired too, in much the same manner.

Smooth, white sands grace the coastline as gentle rollers whiten the shore; Jacksonville Beach is understandably a popular destination

RECOMMENDED WALKS

Guided walking tours of the 50-block historic downtown district of Fernandina Beach on Amelia Island are a must for anyone with an interest in American Victorian architecture. These depart from the Chamber of Commerce at 3pm on Monday and Thursday, May through September (at other times inquire at the Museum of History). If you want to do the tour yourself, pick up a leaflet from the Chamber of Commerce.

SCENIC ROUTES

Follow the bank of the St John's River between Tocoi and Picolata, with views of ancient live oaks with shaggy beards of Spanish moss. Just beyond the road are set some fine riverside mansions, and private fishing and boat jetties protrude into the peaceful river. Spanish moss is an epiphyte (it grows on another plant without harming it) and is related to the pineapple. Why Spanish moss? One explanation likens it to the beards of early Spanish settlers.

Mayport

2 Mayport Naval Station is the navy's fourth largest home port and the largest and busiest naval base in Florida. It is home to mine-sweepers, aircraft carriers, cruisers, frigates and destroyers. Free tours aboard certain ships are available to the public at the weekend. At the mouth of the St John's River is the 300-year-old Mayport fishing village, home to a large commercial shrimp boat fleet. Mayport is not exactly a pretty village, but there is plenty of authentic salty atmosphere to savor, particularly at **Singleton's Seafood Shack** (next to the ferry), where you can also sample the freshly landed catch.

Cross the river on the car ferry to Fort George Island.

Kingsley Plantation

3 Set well back from SR A1A, this is the oldest surviving plantation in Florida, dating back to 1792. Just before the entrance gates are some ruined outbuildings, made of tabby (a primitive oyster-shell concrete), where the plantation slaves lived and raised cotton, sugarcane, corn, black-eyed peas and sweet potatoes. The enthusiastic rangers will tell you about the conditions under which the slaves lived and worked and entertain you with colorful stories of the plantation owners, including Zepheniah Kingsley and his African wife who ruled her slaves with a rod of iron. You can see inside the main house, built in 1817, and around the plantation grounds (by guided tour only Thursday through Monday).

Continue north on SR A1A.

Little Talbot Island

4 Some 5 miles (8km) of wide sand beaches, salt marshes and dunes have been preserved as a state park on this barrier island. Along the 4-mile (6km) nature trail or the ranger-led canoe trail you may catch a glimpse of armadillos, opossums, raccoons, gopher tortoises, frogs and cotton rats. The park is also a particularly good spot for bird-watching, as nearly 200 species are known to inhabit the island.

Continue north on SR A1A to Amelia Island

Seashells, coral and sharks' teeth for sale on Jacksonville Beach. All these wares are common offerings to be found washed up on the shores of Florida

Amelia Island

5 Amelia Island, in the northeastern-most corner of Florida, has the dubious distinction of being the only place in the state to have come under eight flags: French (1562–65), Spanish (1565–1763 and 1783–1821), British (1763–83), Patriots (1812), Green Cross of Florida (1817), Mexican (1817–21), Confederate (1861–62) and American (1821–61 and 1862 to the present).

Equestrian types will love the **Sea Horse Stables**, at the southern tip of the island. This is one of the places on the East Coast where you can ride horseback on the beach, and the wide near-deserted beaches are a perfect setting; by reservation only, tel (904) 261-4878).

Continue on **SR AIA** parallel to the ocean, past **Amelia Island Plantation Resort** and some 13 miles (21km) of unspoiled beaches and dunes, and on to **Fort Clinch State Park**. Built in 1847 and occupied by both Northern and Southern troops during the Civil War, the fort is in an outstanding state of preservation. It features a living history interpretation in which the year is 1864 and the garrison soldiers are going about their daily duties. For an even more atmospheric visit, book one of the candlelight tours given every Friday and Saturday during the summer. (Saturday only during spring and fall); tel (904) 261-4212. You will also find here some of the finest beaches on the island and a nature trail winding through a coastal hammock, where alligators and wading birds can be seen.

🛈 Amelia Island/Fernandina Beach/Yulee Chamber of Commerce, 102 Centre Street, Fernandina Beach

*Return to **SR A1A** and follow it to Centre Street.*

Neat and tidy, cream upon red, the building at the corner of Center and North Second streets, Fernandina Beach

A becalmed sea appears to hold the boats of the Fernandina Beach shrimping fleet in a grip of suspended animation

Fernandina Beach

6 Centre Street is the main artery of the picturesque historic town of Fernandina Beach, and it ends at the shrimp dock. A plaque at the waterfront tells you that this is the birthplace of Florida's shrimping industry. Come here at sunset for a wonderful photo-opportunity. By the dock is the old rail depot (opened in 1899), now the Chamber of Commerce. A walk along colorful Centre Street will soon give you a flavor of the town. Most of the buildings are shops, superbly restored to their original appearance of a century or more ago. Don't miss the **Palace Saloon**. Built in 1878 and a bar since 1903, it is Florida's oldest saloon still on its original site, resembling part Wild West saloon and part Victorian English pub with swing doors, a hand-carved bar, beveled glass windows and elaborate ceiling decoration. Here you can see the Patriot Flag, the shortest-lived of all eight banners to have been hoisted over the island, flying for just one day. Other Victorian gems on Centre Street include the **Three Star Saloon**, the **City Mart**, now home to **Fantastic Fudge** and the **Nassau County Courthouse**. For a complete history tour visit the excellent **Museum of History** on Second Street (off Centre Street), housed in the old county jail. A lively presentation by a museum tour guide precedes a tour of the museum and, if you wish, a walking tour of the area.

SPECIAL TO . . .

6 *Fernandina Beach* If you are a seafood lover or harbor nautical interests, visit Amelia Island's **Isle of Eight Flags Shrimp Festival** on the first weekend in May. This two-and-a-half-day event draws over 125,000 people to a festival of arts, crafts and antiques, a pirate invasion, the Blessing of the Fleet, shrimping demonstrations, a best beard contest and firework displays. The festival is centered on Fernandina Beach's shrimp docks, and visitors are welcomed aboard the working boats.

The stolid, cathedral-like brick bell tower of the University of Florida, Gainsville, is almost painfully abrupt

Leave Amelia Island on **SR A1A** *traveling west, and after 11 miles (18km) turn left onto* **US 17***, and head south to Jacksonville.*

Take the city tour of Jacksonville (see page 106).

From Jacksonville head west on **I-10** *and turn off south at* **US 301***. Continue for 34 miles (55km), then turn right on to* **SR 24** *(Waldo Road).*

Gainesville

7 This large, well-kept city is closely associated with the University of Florida, but it also features a fine historic district and, around the outskirts, some interesting natural features. As you enter the center of town, turn right onto **SR 24/26** (Newberry Road) and right again on NE 6th Avenue to the historic district. The flagship house of the district is the beautifully restored Mediterranean Revival **Thomas Center**, which puts on art exhibits, music and guided tours (closed Saturday). Continue on Newberry Road and turn left on **US 441**, which leads past the elegant red-brick buildings of the university. On the right is the **Florida Museum of Natural History**, the Southeast's largest natural science exhibit. An interesting diversion 2 miles (3km) northwest of town (take **US 441** north, then west on NW 53rd Avenue) takes in the **Devil's Millhopper State Geological Site**. Formed by a collapsed underground cavern, this is basically a huge chasm, 120 feet (37m) deep and 500 feet (152m) wide with its own ecosystem, supporting animals more common to the ravines of the Appalachian Mountains and dozens of plant species found nowhere else in Florida. There is a visitor center and guided walks are conducted on Saturday mornings. More exotic plants, including the largest collection of bamboo in Florida, can be enjoyed just south at **Kanapaha Botanical Garden** (SW 63rd Boulevard, just off I-75). Near here at Archer Road (**SR 24**) is the **Fred Bear Museum**. This is an unusual collection of archery and hunting artifacts from all over the world together with natural history displays, several of these being hunting trophies.

From the Florida Museum of Natural History continue south on **US 441** *for 10 miles (17 km).*

Paynes Prairie State Preserve

8 During the late 17th century this vast 18,000-acre (7,285-hectare) savannah was occupied by the largest cattle ranch in Spanish Florida. In the 18th century Seminole Indians settled here, and it is thought that the prairie is named after King Payne, a Seminole chief. There is a visitor center and an observation tower where you can watch waterfowl and wading birds. One mile (1.5km) southwest of the park is the small hamlet of **Micanopy** (pronounced

Mik-An-o-pee). A white trading post grew up here in 1821, making this one of the oldest settlements in Florida. Its picturesque main street is lined with moss-draped live oaks and historical buildings, of which around 20 are antique shops. In the fall some 200 dealers converge here for an annual antique fair.

Continue east from Micanopy on SR 346 for 5 miles (8km). Turn right (south) on to SR 325 and continue for 3½ miles (5km).

Cross Creek

9 'Cross Creek is a bend in a country road by land and the flowing of Lochloosa Lake into Orange Lake by water.' So began Marjorie Kinnan Rawlings' story of her life at Cross Creek. Even if you have never heard of the 1939 Pulitzer prize-winning author (*The Yearling*), the countryside around here and her 1890s home (now a state historic site) are still lovely, unspoiled placed to visit (closed Tuesdays and Wednesdays). Marjorie Kinnan Rawlings lived at Cross Creek from 1928 to 1941 continuously, and intermittently until her death in 1953. Here the land and the 'Cracker' people (original white rural settlers) inspired her to become one of the greatest names in 20th-century American literature.

Continue southeast on SR 325 for 5 miles (8km) to Island Grove, then turn left on to US 301. Head north for 8 miles (13km) to Hawthorne and turn right onto SR 20. Head east for 30 miles (48km), to Palatka.

The magnificent colonial façade of Casa Rodriquez on St George Street, at the heart of St Augustine's Spanish Quarter

Ravine State Gardens, Palatka

10 The steep ravines created by waters flowing from the St John's River, now dry except for a spring-fed creek, are home to delightful wild gardens crossed by old wooden suspension bridges. A 3-mile (5km) loop road enables you to see the gardens without leaving your car, but walking is definitely recommended.

Follow US17 east across the river and turn left on to SR 207 to return to St Augustine.

St Augustine–Jacksonville Beach **58 (93)**
Jacksonville Beach–Mayport **8 (13)**
Mayport–Kingsley Plantation **1 (2)**
Kingsley Plantation–Little Talbot Island **3 (5)**
Little Talbot Island–Amelia Island **8 (13)**
Amelia Island–Fernandina Beach **13 (21)**
Fernandina Beach–Jacksonville **33 (53)**
Jacksonville–Gainesville **66 (106)**
Gainesville–Paynes Prairie State Preserve **10 (16)**
Paynes Prairie State Preserve–Cross Creek **8 (13)**
Cross Creek–Ravine Gardens **44 (71)**
Ravine Gardens–St Augustine **30 (48)**

FOR HISTORY BUFFS

2 *Jacksonville Beach* **Fort Caroline** was the site of the first confrontation between France and Spain for supremacy over Florida in 1565. The French sent a fleet out from the fort to attack the Spanish, but it was wrecked by storms, leaving their colony vulnerable. The Spanish, led by Pedro Menéndez (founder of St Augustine), sacked the fort, killing 140 of its inhabitants and capturing the other 70. The ship-wrecked French sailors were shown no mercy by Menéndez: at the place that still bears the name Matanzas (Slaughter) Bay, near St Augustine, some 200 to 300 of them were massacred. A replica of the fort and a memorial stand on the original site some 10 miles (16km) east of Jacksonville.

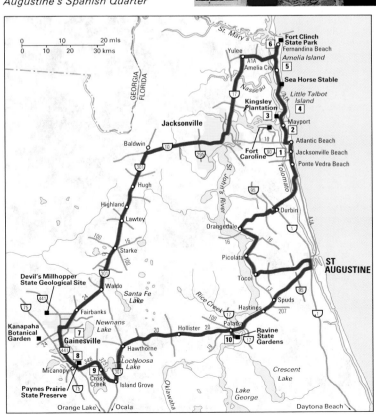

JACKSONVILLE CITY

Anheuser-Busch Brewery
Jacksonville Zoological Park
Jacksonville Landing • Riverwalk
Museum of Science and History (MOSH)
Cummer Gallery of Art • Jacksonville Art Museum

At 841 square miles (2,178sq km) Jacksonville is a large city. Don't let that discourage you, though, as its major visitor attractions are clustered conveniently close to each other around the center. Lately, the downtown area has enhanced one of its most vital assets, the St John's River, by placing on either bank a boardwalk and a shopping and restaurant complex. These developments, brightly lit at night and complemented by the city's spectacular skyline, give a festive air to the river and have been a great success. When it comes to visitor attractions, it is a case of quality rather than mere quantity. The zoo is highly regarded nationally, the Museum of Science and History is the finest of its kind in Florida, and the Cummer Gallery is one of the state's hidden gems. By night Jacksonville has all the attractions and cultural diversity that you would expect of a major city, including the oldest civic theater (the Theater Jacksonville) in the country. Regular sporting and festive events of national importance are also staged in the city.

🛈 Jacksonville Convention and Visitors Bureau, 6 East Bay Street, Suite 200 (adjacent to Jacksonville Landing parking lot)

If you are continuing the tour of the northeast follow US 17 for 21 miles (34km) south and turn right on Busch Drive. Alternatively, from the center of town head north on US 17 and turn left on Busch Drive.

FOR CHILDREN

5 *Museum of Science and History* **Kidspace** at the Museum of Science and History is designed to be a child's first experience in scientific learning. It features its own phone system, face-painting stations, a treehouse where kids can operate their own puppet theater, large soft-sculpture building blocks and a dynamic water table. Adults must be accompanied by a child up to 48 inches tall (122cm). Older children will also enjoy the evening laser shows.

Anheuser-Busch Brewery

1 If you have ever wondered what they put into your Budweiser and how, a free tour of this gigantic brewery should slake your thirst for knowledge (closed Sunday). After the tour adults can sample the famous 'King of Beers' in the hospitality room (soft drinks also available for drivers and those under 21).

Return to US 17, follow it for about 1½ miles (2.5km) south to Heckscher Drive East (exit 124-A) and turn left and then right.

Jacksonville Zoological Park

2 One of the oldest and most famous attractions in the city, the zoo

---

Members of the African delegation take to the shade at Jacksonville Zoological Park

(established in 1914) boasts over 700 species. Highlights include the 11-acre (4-hectare) African veldt where eland, kudu and ostrich roam freely, the new Okavango Trail, a boardwalk through pinewoods where animals native to southern Africa can be seen, a large outdoor aviary and rare white rhinos. Most of the animals can be viewed in a near-natural state, separated from the public by moats instead of cages. **Chimporama, Okavango Petting Zoo** and elephant rides delight children, and train rides tour the full 61-acre (25-hectare) site.

Return to US 17 and follow it south into downtown. Park just before the Main Street Bridge at Jacksonville Landing.

Jacksonville Landing

3 This attractive riverside complex is home to dozens of specialty shops, fast food and fine dining, nightclubs and a one-room **Maritime Museum** chock-full of model ships. Behind the complex tower the giants of the city, including the 37-story **Independent Life Building** (tours available), while ahead is the busy St John's River. The splendid design of the Landing is by the Rouse Company, also responsible for Miami's Bayside Marketplace, Faneuil Hall in Boston and the Harborplace in Baltimore. Regular festivities and ever-present street entertainers ensure that there is never a dull moment. Immediately to the west, the dramatic Greek Revival-style building, with 14 massive columns and three pediments, is the **Prime Osborne Convention Center**. Formerly the grandiose Union Terminal railroad station, built in 1919, it now functions as an exhibition and meeting hall.

Take a water-taxi across the river.

Riverwalk

4 This old-fashioned boardwalk, just over a mile (2km) long and 20 feet (6m) wide, is lined with restaurants, food vendors and boat rentals (including a Venetian gondola). Several major annual events are staged here, including an arts and crafts festival in May, when some 50,000 people tread the boards.

At the beginning of the Riverwalk is the city's premier museum.

Museum of Science and History (MOSH)

5 This large museum is neatly divided into discrete sections. The **Living World** is home to the museum's live animal collection and includes a 1,200-US-gallon (4,540-liter) aquarium and an aviary overlooking the Hixon Courtyard, a piece of tropical hammock in the middle of downtown. The **Science Center** features the very latest in hands-on exhibits, with over 40 science PODS (personally operated discovery stations) plus the state-of-the-art **Alexander Brest Planetarium**. This is said to be the finest planetarium chamber in the US with the best possible sound system. You can not only hear but feel the launch of a shuttle and the explosion of a star. For more life in space visit **Asteroid Biosphere 3**, which re-creates a space colony in the aster-oid belt. In addition to all this, there is **Kidspace** (see For Children), outstanding traveling exhibitions and a waterside café to relax in. Step outside the museum to

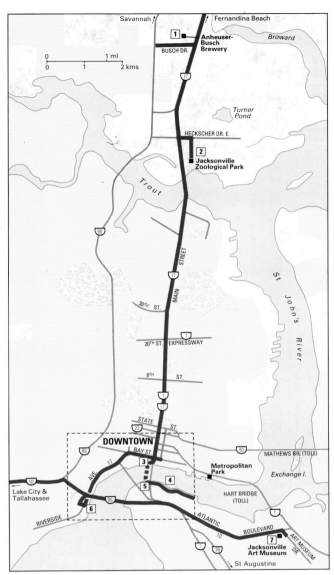

Children admire their caricatures in a curved mirror at the Museum of Science and History

see the spectacular **Friendship Fountain**. This sprays 17,000 US gal-lons (64,000 liters) of water 120 feet (37m) into the air every minute and is particularly impressive when lit at night.

Return to your car. Follow the north bank of the river south on Riverside Avenue and continue a few blocks south after passing under I-95 (the approach to the Fuller-Warren Bridge).

Cummer Gallery of Art

6 This outstanding fine arts museum and cultural center exhibits a per-manent collection of over 2,000 items in 11 galleries. Of special note is one of the world's largest and rarest collections of early Meissen porcelain, plus some fine 17th-century Dutch and Flemish paintings and tapestries. Beautiful Florentine gardens lead to the river.

Cross the Fuller-Warren Bridge (I-95), and after 1 mile (1.5km), turn left onto Atlantic Boulevard and right onto Art Museum Drive.

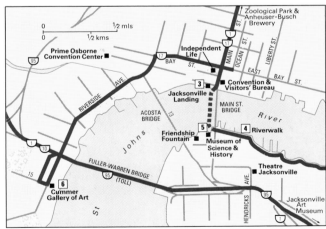

Jacksonville Art Museum

7 The city's oldest museum stages both contemporary and classic art exhibitions. The collection of Chinese porcelains and rare artifacts from the pre-Columbian era are its highlights.

Continue the northeast tour (see page 104) by recrossing the Fuller-Warren Bridge and picking up I-10 west. Go south at US 301. Alternatively, return to St Augustine on US 1 or I-95.

SPECIAL TO ...

The three-day **Jacksonville Jazz Festival** in early October is the largest free jazz event in the US and draws crowds of 130,000 at Metropolitan Park. The park is also a venue for a **Spring MusicFest** in late April/early May, a country music festival in April and two weeks of Shakespeare's plays in September.

THE PANHANDLE

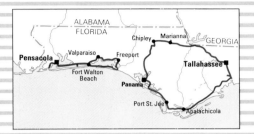

If peninsular Florida is the pan, then the long thin strip bordering Georgia and Alabama is the panhandle. This is the other Florida, where glades and palms are replaced by rolling hills and pine and oak forests, which resemble the countryside of New York rather than the swamplands of southern Florida. Slick shopping malls give way to a countrified selection of collectibles, and the mention of Disney Animatronics will just get you a good ol' Southern guffaw. This Florida is not only a geographical extension of the southern states, it is also a cultural extension of southern Alabama and Georgia – the heart of old Dixie. Just look at the menu for confirmation – grits, hush puppies, catfish, black-eyed beans and chitlins, served in establishments with names such as Po' Folks. Snowbirds and retirees are still thick on the ground in the northwest, but Europeans are largely absent and you are more likely to meet families from other Southern states and Canada.

The vacation seasons here are also different from southern Florida. As the rest of the state begins to swelter, the cooler panhandle summer season is just beginning. While the region's beaches cater for a burgeoning tourist trade, the northern hinterland is an area of slow, meandering rivers, lakes, springs and even caverns. There are, of course, parallels with southern Florida: Panama City Beach is the Daytona Beach of the north, Pensacola rivals St Augustine for historical heritage, and Wakulla Springs resembles an earlier, less commercialized version of Silver Springs. The region's Southern accent is most pronounced around the green canopied roads of Tallahassee, but despite the well-publicized fact that this region still harbors the largest concentration of antebellum plantations in the US, don't expect to encounter too many *Gone With the Wind* fantasies on the Florida side of the state line.

The Gulf Coast beaches of the Panhandle are often called collectively the Miracle Strip, a wry reference to the 'miraculous' price hikes experienced when the area's tourism potential was discovered in the years following World War II. The major resorts that have grown up here, however, are cheap and cheerful and the real treasure is the sugar-white sand — the result of quartz crystals from the Appalachian Mountains that have been broken down, washed, bleached, ground and polished by the action of the Gulf waters. The beaches and the barrier islands as far east as Destin are part of the Gulf Islands National Seashore, and are vigilantly protected by the National Park Service. The beaches too have a soubriquet — The Emerald Coast, a perfect name on a sunny summer day when the sparkling green-blue waters lap the snowy white shores.

Tour 15
The tour starts at the state capital, Tallahassee. The Capitol Complex is the hub of modern-day Tallahassee's role as lawmaker and administrator to the state, and also gives a fine historical introduction to the region. The city itself is full of cultural and historical interest and is temptingly close to the lovely Georgia town of Thomasville. The route west passes through rolling green hills to pristine state parks, featuring caverns and a waterfall before heading to the coast. Panama City Beach is a lively, highly commercialized beach resort with plenty of action for youngsters and teenagers. Port St Joe and Apalachicola are complete contrasts — the former a sleepy, faded fishing village, the latter an important fishing port famed for its oysters. Wakulla Springs is an unforgettable trip down the river into Old Florida.

Tour 16
The city of Pensacola is a must for history buffs, with its streets a living legacy of the period from Colonial times to the Depression. The city is not cocooned in its own past, however; the National Museum of Naval Aviation and the adjacent resort of Pensacola Beach provide ample outlets for those whose interests are more athletic than academic. More beautiful unspoiled beaches can be found along the protected Gulf Islands National Seashore, and the resort of Fort Walton Beach is another good all-round resort, with a US Air Force museum for fans of flying.

The diversity of the beach communities of the South Walton area ranges from Seaside, a newly created, pretty Cape Cod-style resort, to Destin, a busy fishing charter port and vacation center over 150 years old.

A forest of masts punctuates the morning sky above silent waters at Blue Water Bay

The emerging sun fires the morning's sky and bursts through the misty swamp

2 days – 288 miles (463km)

TALLAHASSEE & BEYOND

A sea-hardened veteran of the Apalachicola fishing fleet, with bow held high, takes a moment to survey its surroundings

Tallahassee ● Capitol Complex
Union Bank/LeMoyne ● Florida Caverns State Park
Falling Waters State Recreation Area
Panama City ● Port St Joe ● Apalachicola
San Marcos de Apalache State Historic Site
Wakulla Springs State Park ● Tallahassee

As you gaze across Tallahassee from the observatory of the towering new Capitol Building, it seems odd that this small, relatively quiet town should be the capital of such a dynamic state. Tallahassee was chosen as capital in 1824 because it lay midway on a long and dangerous journey between the principal towns of St Augustine and Pensacola, and despite the fact that half the population of Florida now lives south of Orlando, it has still managed to legitimize its status. In many ways the character of the area has changed little since the state constitution was first drafted here back in 1838. The countryside has retained much of its natural rolling greenery and timeless features such as Wakulla Springs, while the towns, big and small, still possess that laid-back southern atmosphere more associated with Georgia and Alabama, which lie just a few miles north. Tallahassee is in many ways a modern city with a nevertheless keen respect for its past; it is the antithesis of the port of Panama City, which is crudely embracing budget tourism. Away from the Miracle Strip, however, you will probably feel less like a tourist and more like a traveler in a land that seems only distantly related to Mickey's Florida.

RECOMMENDED WALKS

There are several fine nature walks along this route ranging from a 1-mile (1.5km) trail at the Tallahassee Junior Museum to a 7-mile (11km) hike at Torreya State Park. The two trails at Wakulla Springs, each 2 miles (3km) long, are particularly worthwhile, moving through abundant birdlife, Spanish moss-draped trees and a generally ancient landscape.

Park your car and you can explore most of downtown Tallahassee on foot. Alternatively, jump aboard a trolley car; the service runs a small circuit around central downtown.

Capitol Complex

1 This administrative complex, the historic old seat of Florida's government and its 22-story successor, makes for a good introduction to Tallahassee (which means 'old town'). The Old Capitol is just as you would expect, a handsome classical-style building with a green cupola. It was built in 1845 but has been restored, both externally and internally, to its 1902 appearance. It includes the Supreme Court, the House of Representatives and Senate Chambers and the Governor's Suite; all are open to the public. Other offices in the building have been converted into museum space, and a visit is well worthwhile. Access to the new State Capitol, erected in 1977, is obviously limited, but there are frequent free guided tours to certain parts of the building, and the 22-story observation deck is open during office hours. The ground floor also holds an extensive state-wide visitor information center. The Capitol really comes to life from April into June, which is when the legislative sessions take place. By law all such meetings are open to the public, and guided tours will tell you what is happening. Adjacent to the Capitol is the Veterans Memorial, its twin granite towers flying the Stars and Stripes, erected in honor of Florida's Vietnam veterans.

Cross Monroe Street and a few yards away is the Union Bank.

Union Bank/LeMoyne Art Gallery

2 Built in 1841, this is Florida's oldest surviving bank building and today houses a museum of banking and daily life (Monday to Saturday). Turn left at Gadsden Street and a block north is the LeMoyne Art Gallery, the city's center for the visual arts, housed in a small, well-proportioned 1853 mansion. One block west, turn right onto Calhoun Street; here you will find many of the city's oldest homes, most dating between 1830 and 1880. Park Avenue, heading west off Calhoun, also features many historic buildings (look on the left-hand side of the street). Walk up Park Avenue, turn left back towards the Capitol, and at the rear of the complex is the **Museum of Florida History**. This well-designed modern museum traces the story of Florida with exhibits like a 9-foot (2.7m) mastodon (from Wakulla Springs), Spanish galleon treasure, Civil War battle flags, a reconstructed steamboat, and the 'tin-can' camper tourists of the 1920s. Step outside the museum to the reconstructed center of historical downtown, **Adams Street Commons**. Just along Duval Street is **The Columns**, the city's oldest building, dating from 1830. It is now the headquarters of the Chamber of Commerce, and is partly open to the public as a visitor information center. Tallahassee also boasts Florida State University, and just west of the Capitol you can visit the **FSU Gallery and Museum**. Located at the corner of Copeland and Call streets, this hosts touring exhibitions, plus a permanent collection that includes 20th-century American and

The tree-shrouded structure of the classically inspired Capitol Complex, Tallahassee

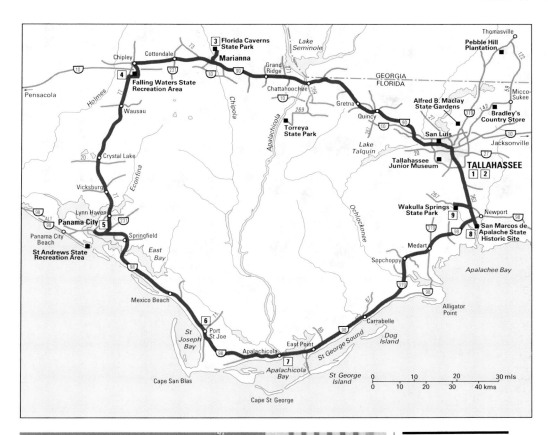

SPECIAL TO...

To catch a glimpse of the gracious antebellum *Gone With the Wind* Deep South, you will have to cross the state border into Georgia. Fortunately, one of Georgia's finest small towns, **Thomasville**, is only 35 miles (56km) north of Tallahassee; even closer—just 20 miles (32km) north—is the elegant **Pebble Hill Plantation**. Complete your day by returning on **SR 59** to Centerville Road and dropping in at **Bradley's Country Store**. Country smoked sausage and other southern cooking specialties have made the store a local legend since 1927. (Note: driving outside Florida could invalidate your car rental insurance policy; check before crossing the state line.)

SCENIC ROUTES

The road from Tallahassee to Chipley, skirting the foothills of the Appalachian Mountains, is quite unlike anywhere else in Florida, with rolling wooded hills and green ravines. Tallahassee itself boasts a number of 'canopy roads', where moss-draped live oaks reach right across and touch over the street. The best of these are to the north and include Centerville Road, which is en route to Bradley's Country Store (see Special To).

A sunbather quietly replenishes her tan at Shipwreck Island, Panama City Beach, while all hell lets loose behind her

*Drive 1 mile (1.5km) west to pick up **SR 77** and head south for 42 miles (68km). Turn right onto **US 98** into Panama City.*

Panama City

5 Panama City Beach, some 5 miles (8km) south of the town proper, is the major resort on the northern Gulf coast, a busy, brash place popular with college students and Southern families on a tight budget (hence its nickname 'The Redneck Riviera'). From May to September, the busy season, hotel rooms are fully booked and almost permanent traffic clogs US 98 (Alt), which leads to the beaches. Unfortunately, outside this period the major attractions close down for the winter. The beaches along this strip of coastline, however, are some of the very best in the state. Made up of 99 per cent quartz crystal, the sand looks and feels like powdered sugar and actually squeaks as you walk on it.

Miracle Strip Amusement Park is the biggest man-made attraction in town, with over 30 fairground-style rides and one of the country's most

The harvesters of the ocean bed hide, almost ashamedly, behind a veritable mountain of discarded oyster shells – the product of many fishing trips

16th-century Dutch paintings, Japanese prints and pre-Columbian pieces.

Five miles (8km) northeast of Tallahassee is the outstanding **Alfred B Maclay State Gardens** (1 mile/1.5km) north of I-10 on US 319). The star blooms are the 100 varieties of camellias and the 50 kinds of azaleas, but another 160 exotic species complement these. The season is from January through April, with the peak in mid- to late March. During this period the **Maclay House**, furnished as it was in the 1920s, is also open. The gardens encircle a beautifully landscaped lake where you can see alligators, turtles and migrating waterfowl, and in the park's woodlands over 150 species of wildlife have been recorded. You might like to combine a visit to the gardens with an excursion to Thomasville (see Special To).

*From downtown head west on Brevard Avenue/Quincy Highway (**US 90**) through Quincy and Chattahoochee for some 65 miles (104km) to Marianna. Turn right onto **SR 167** and head north for 3 miles (5km).*

Florida Caverns State Park

3 There are many similar limestone cave formations in Florida, but because of the state's high water table this is the only significant network of caves that is not flooded. The largest and most impressive caves are lit and open to the public for ranger-guided tours. Sodastraws, stalagmites, stalactites, draperies (resembling petrified curtains) and calcite formations of all shapes and sizes provide a memorable visit. The park also offers swimming, a horse trail (no rentals) and canoe rentals.

*Return to **US 90** and continue west for 19 miles (31km) to Chipley. Turn left onto **SR 77A** and head south for 3 miles (5km).*

Falling Waters State Recreation Area

4 The highlight of this park is a 67-foot (20m) waterfall, another geological feature rarely found in this state. It plunges into a sinkhole some 100 feet (30m) deep and 20 feet (6m) wide. This underutilized park also offers picnicking and nature trails that feature many uncommon plants and unusual geological formations.

BACK TO NATURE

Tallahassee Aside from beautiful Maclay State Gardens and pristine Wakulla Springs, you may like to take a short detour off this route to **Torreya State Park**, some 17 miles (27km) south of Chatahoochee on **US 90**). The landscape here is more akin to Georgia's Appalachians than Florida, with verdant high bluffs rising 150 feet (46m) above the river. The park takes its name from a rare tree that grows only along these river bluffs. As a bonus, tours are conducted through the historic Gregory House, built in 1849.

heart-stopping roller coasters. **Ship-wreck Island**, adjacent, is a large water park with a giant wave pool, a white-water tube ride, a 35mph (56km/h) racing slide, a 1,600-foot (488m) Lazy River ride and several themed areas in which to simply sunbathe. If you are more serious about your water thrills, there is every kind of watersport back on the beach, and the area is well known for its diving schools. The other major attraction here is **Gulf World marine park**. Bottle-nosed dolphins and sea lions star in entertaining shows, and there is a shark pool, a penguin exhibit and a dolphin petting pool. Finally there is the **Museum of Man in the Sea**. Here you can see some of the numerous imaginative devices that would-be sea explorers have invented over the centuries to allow themselves to breathe, move and work beneath the waves. The most scenic beach is **St Andrews State Recreation Area**, located at the end of Thomas Road/US 98 (Alt), where you can also fish or wander along the nature trail. Boats leave from here for an uninhabited natural barrier isle, named **Shell Island** after the numerous types of shells buried beneath its silvery sands. Other charters will take you sea fishing, dolphin feeding or touring the Gulf floor by glass-bottom boat.

☐ Visitor Information Center, Front Beach Road

*Head southeast on **US 98** for 39 miles (63km).*

Port St Joe

6 St Joseph, as it used to be called, was created in 1835 and soon grew to be a booming port with a population of some 12,000. In 1838 it secured a certain degree of immortality by being the place where the first Florida state constitution was drafted, but by 1844—wracked by yellow fever, economic problems and finally an almighty hurricane—the town had dwindled to insignificance. Visit the **Constitutional Convention State Museum** to learn about this historic charter, and the sad story of how proud St Joseph was reduced to plain St Joe.

*Continue east on **US 98** for 22 miles (35km).*

Apalachicola

7 An important Confederate port during the Civil War, this much restored fishing village has a New England flavor to it and is famous for its oyster beds. The vast majority of Florida's oysters come from here, as does half the state's shellfish, so you are always assured of the freshest seafood in the local restaurants. The beautifully renovated **Gibson Hotel**, dating from 1910, is a local landmark and probably the most characterful place to stay on this route. If you are just passing through, try the restaurant and lounge to sample the local oysters and its romantic turn-of-the-century ambience. The town's other claim to fame lies with Dr John

FOR HISTORY BUFFS

Tallahassee Three miles (5km) west of downtown Tallahassee is the **San Luis Archaeological and Historic Site**, the location of an important 17th-century Spanish and Apalachee Indian village. Spanish explorers came here in 1656, building a fort and a church and retaining the huge thatched circular Indian gathering place. Unfortunately, the village was burned and abandoned by its inhabitants in the face of hostile British and Creek forces in 1704, so there is now little to see. Free guided tours will interpret the site for you, however, and there is also a visitor center (housed in a fine 1938 mansion) with several exhibits.

Gorrie, who, during the early 1800s, served not only as town physician but also as postmaster, city treasurer, councilman and bank director. His concern for his yellow-fever patients led him to invent an ice-making machine for cooling rooms, thus paving the way for air-conditioning. A replica of his invention is housed in the **John Gorrie State Museum** on 6th Street, off **US 98**.

*Continue east for 33 miles (53km) on **US 98**, then fork left, away from the coast, heading north on **US 319**. Continue north, then east for 17 miles (27km) before rejoining **US 98**. Continue northeast on **US 98** for 13 miles (21km), then turn right onto **SR 363** and head south for 2 miles (3km).*

San Marcos de Apalache State Historic Site

8 This area was first discovered by Europeans in 1528, when Panfilo de Narvaez arrived at what is now St Mark's with 300 Conquistadores. Here he established a boatyard and launched the first ships made by white men in the New World. The fort, first built on the site in 1679, was destroyed and twice rebuilt; the most recent stone fort was occupied by Confederate forces in 1861. The museum here displays finds from the area and relates the colorful history of San Marcos.

*Return north on **SR 363** for 2 miles (3km), cross **US 98** and continue on **SR 363** for a further 3 miles (5km), then turn left onto **SR 267**.*

Wakulla Springs State Park

9 Variously and romantically translated as 'breast of life' or 'mysteries of strange waters', Wakulla claims one of the largest and deepest freshwater springs in the world. Peak flow has been measured at over 14,000 US gallons (53,000 liters) per second. Glass-bottom boats are the major visitor attraction here, and when the water is clear you

Resplendently colored ducks ply the waters of Wakulla Springs. Lush, vibrant, subtropical swampland comes forward to define the pool's edges

can peer down through the crystal waters to the entrance of the spring cavern some 100 feet (30m) below. The cave has been explored to a distance of 4,200 feet (1,280m), and finds include the remains of a giant mastodon (now in Tallahassee's Museum of Florida History). The two scenic boat tours, similar to those at better-known Silver Springs (see Tour 12) cruise through a breathtaking primeval Florida riverscape. It was here that several of the early Johnny Weissmuller *Tarzan* movies were filmed. *The Creature from the Black Lagoon* was also shot here, though today the only creature likely to alarm you is 'Henry the Pole-Vaulting Fish', who leaps out of the water on command as one of the boat captain's *tours de force*. The river is a birdwatcher's delight, with herons and egrets, black and turkey vultures, anhingas, kites, ospreys, bald eagles, limpkins and purple gallinules; turtles and alligators abound. Do not miss visiting **Wakulla Springs Lodge and Conference Center**. Built in 1937, it includes many original Spanish features, notably its tiled doorway and arches and Moorish grilled doors. The dining room, seemingly caught in a 1950s time warp, is acclaimed for its choice of traditional regional dishes. Its Southern cooking is well worth sampling, particularly as your park admission fee will then be waived (boat tours charged separately).

*Return to **SR 363**, and head north for 13 miles (21km) to return to Tallahassee.*

THE PENSACOLA GULF COAST

What fisherman would not envy the stretch of coast this patient angler has on Pensacola Beach?

ℹ Pensacola Visitor Information Center, East Gregory Street (by north end of Pensacola Bay Bridge)

Pensacola's three historic districts are best explored on foot. Leave your car at the Historic Pensacola Village parking lot on East Zaragoza Street.

Historic Pensacola Village

1 This fine collection of museums and interpretive houses lies at the heart of the Seville Square Historic District. If you would like to visit the museums, buy an all-inclusive admission ticket before starting your tour. Walk west along Church Street to the outstanding **T T Wentworth Jr Florida State Museum**, which is housed in an imposing Italian Renaissance Revival structure built in 1908 as the Pensacola City Hall. It contains some 30,000 items of local and regional interest and is the largest collection ever donated to the State of Florida by an individual. Walk back along Church Street to the **Museum of Industry**, which features 19th-century local industry memorabilia, and in particular relates to the west Florida lumber boom of the 1890s. Opposite is the **Museum of Commerce**, with an 1890s streetscape comprising a barbershop, a toy store, a print shop, a hardware store and a pharmacy. Diagonally opposite on Barrack Street is the early 19th-century **Julee Cottage**. This was owned by Julee Panton, one of the region's pioneering free black women, and is now home to a **Museum of Black History**. From the same period, across the street, is the French Colonial **Creole Charles Lavallé House**. Step inside to admire its hand-made antiques and provincial furniture and a fully equipped cooking hearth. Opposite the house is **Old Christ Church**, built in 1832, now serving as a local museum. Straight ahead is Seville Square, where several shops, restaurants and offices occupy old properties and continue the quarter's historic traditions. On the Adam Street side, look in at **Dorr House**, built in 1871 for a wealthy lumber merchant and fully furnished with ornate Victorian antiques.

You can complete seeing the main properties in the Seville Historic District one block east of Seville Square.

Pensacola ● Historic Pensacola Village
Seville, Palafox and North Hill
National Museum of Aviation ● Gulf Breeze Zoo
Santa Rosa Island ● Fort Walton Beach
Eden State Gardens ● Seaside
Destin ● Okaloosa Island Beaches
Pensacola

Pensacola has the distinction of being the last town in Florida as you head west into Alabama. It also likes to call itself Florida's First Place City, on account of its lengthy history. This began in 1559 (six years before St Augustine was founded), when Tristan de Luna settled a colony of around 1,500 people at Pensacola Bay. Had it not been for a devastating hurricane that all but destroyed the settlement, Pensacola would today be acclaimed as the oldest city in Florida. As it was, de Luna abandoned the colony some two years after he first arrived, and Pensacola was not rediscovered for almost two centuries. Since then, however, it has been a key strategic port for five different countries—Spain, France, Britain, the Confederacy and the US (hence another nickname, The City of Five Flags). You can see the mark that all these allegiances have left as you wander the city's historic districts and several museums. Modern Pensacola's claim to fame is as the home of the nation's oldest naval air station, and as a result you can enjoy one of the finest air and space museums in the world. Away from the city and its brash beach resort lies some of Florida's finest, whitest sand.

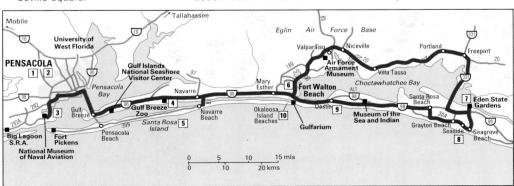

National Museum of Aviation

3 This outstanding museum is home to one of the country's largest and finest historic collections of Navy, Marine Corps and Coast Guard aircraft, plus the very latest high-tech supersonic jets and space vehicles. The stunning seven-story glass and steel entrance atrium features four A-4 Skyhawks belonging to the famous Blue Angels precision flying team, which is based at the adjacent US Naval Air Station. Other exhibits range from the NC-4 Flying Boat, which in 1919 became the first plane to fly the Atlantic, to a replica of the Skylab Command Module. Budding 'top guns' can strap themselves into the cockpit simulator of a modern jet fighter.

*Return by the same route via Main Street onto the Bayfront Parkway and cross the Pensacola Bay Bridge (**US 98**) to Gulf Breeze. Follow the Gulf Breeze Parkway (**US 98**) east for a further 8 miles (13km).*

Gulf Breeze Zoo and Botanical Gardens

4 There are over 500 animals here including lions, tigers, giraffes and Colossus, the world's largest captive gorilla, all in naturally landscaped environments. Exotic birds and other creatures entertain daily during the summer, and there is a children's petting zoo and animal nursery room.

*Continue east on **US 98**, then, just after Navarre, turn right onto **SR 87** and cross the Intracoastal Waterway, 12 miles (19km).*

Santa Rosa Island

5 This long skinny barrier island, part of Gulf Islands National Seashore, boasts miles of beautiful white quartz sand. To the west are the busy, unattractive resort of Pensacola Beach and the quiet historical site of Fort Pickens. Navarre Beach, in the center of the island, is a small relaxed resort; immediately east is a sand-duned wilderness.

Return to the mainland and head east for 16 miles (26km).

Fort Walton Beach

6 The atmosphere in this medium-size resort town lies somewhere between the brashness of Panama City and the calm of Pensacola. Historical associations include the Indian Temple Mound Museum (on US 98) which traces 10,000 years of local Native American life, including a 3,500-year-old temple. Fort Walton is most strongly associated with Eglin Air Force Base, which takes up a massive 700 square miles (1,813sq km) northeast of town; you can visit the base at certain times of the year. Adjacent (open all year round) is the impressive US Air Force Armament Museum. Here you can see the enormous F-105 Thunderchief, the SR-71 Blackbird Spy Plane and a whole arsenal of flying weaponry.

BACK TO NATURE

Pensacola The major conservation feature of this area is **Gulf Islands National Seashore**, which protects 150 square miles (388sq km) of barrier islands. The information center is located east of Gulf Breeze on **US 98**, but for the best overview visit the observation tower at **Big Lagoon State Recreation Area** (SR 292A, 10 miles/16km southwest of Pensacola). In the grounds of the University of West Florida in Pensacola is the **Edward Ball Nature Trail**, a 2½-mile (4km) boardwalk over a wetlands area.

FOR HISTORY BUFFS

5 *Santa Rosa Island* If you are not worn out after walking around Pensacola's historic districts, visit **Fort Pickens** on the western tip of Santa Rosa Island. Built as protection for the Pensacola naval shipyard in 1829, its huge guns, which saw little action, are still in place. The famous Apache chieftain Geronimo was held here from 1886 to 1888, and was joined by three of his wives and his children. You can see the tiny cell where he was kept prisoner.

FOR CHILDREN

When the historic districts of old Pensacola start to get a little dry for young ones, take them along to the **Discovery Gallery** at the **T T Wentworth Museum**, where they can enjoy some hands-on fun. Older children will love the simulators and aviation hardware at the **Air Force Armament Museum**, while the amusement parks at Pensacola Beach and Destin are perennial family favorites.

Seville, Palafox and North Hill Districts

2 Here are the **Musicians' Union Building** (circa 1880) and **Lee House** (1866), both on South Alcaniz Street, the **William Fordham House** (circa 1892) and **Mary Perry House** (circa 1883), both on East Zaragoza Street, and the **Barkley House** (circa 1825) on South Florida Blanca Street.

Walk back towards the parking lot on Zaragoza Street and at the corner of Jefferson Street is the **Pensacola Museum of Art**, housed in the old City Jail, built in 1908. Continue and turn right onto Palafox Street. This was the main thoroughfare of old Pensacola's commercial area. Buildings of interest (from south to north) include: the **Escambia County Courthouse**, an elaborate 1887 Renaissance Revival structure; the **Empire Building**, Florida's tallest skyscraper (at 10 stories) when completed in 1909; and the **Saenger Theatre**, a 1925 vaudeville theater.

Continue north on Palafox Street for four blocks, and at Wright Street you enter the North Hill Preservation District. The 500 homes in this upper-middle class residential quarter, developed between the 1870s and the 1930s, comprise one of the state's most complete historic districts. Continue past the site of old **Fort George** at La Rua Street to Lee Square, where a 50-foot (15m) obelisk was dedicated to the Confederacy in 1891. Continue north for two blocks, turn left on Strong Street and right onto North Baylen Street. The 1896 **Charles H Turner House** and the superb Queen Anne-style **McCreary House** (1900) lie almost opposite each other. Follow Baylen Street south to return to your car.

*Head south on Palafox Street one block to Main Street. Head west and turn left onto Barrancas Avenue (**SR 292**). Follow this for 3 miles (5km) and turn left on Navy Boulevard/Duncan Road (**SR 295**) to cross the Bayou Grande. Follow Duncan Road to Hovey Road, 7 miles (11km).*

Hooked but not landed – a game fish throws itself into the air in an effort to gain freedom

ⓘ Fort Walton Beach Chamber of Commerce, 34 Miracle Strip Parkway

*Take **SR 85** north to Valparaiso and turn right onto **SR 20**. Continue east for 23 miles (37km) to Freeport, turn right onto **US 331** and head south for 10 miles (16km). Turn left onto **US 98** and head east for 3 miles (5km). Turn left on **SR 395**.*

Eden State Gardens

7 The highlight of these isolated gardens is the fine late 19th-century **Wesley Mansion**, which belonged to a wealthy family in the lumber business. Variously described as anything from antebellum to Greek Revival, it is a mix of styles, with antiques and furnishings dating as far back as the 17th century. The best time to visit the lovely grounds is during March, when the azaleas and dogwood are in full bloom.

*Return on **SR 395**, crossing **US 98**, 2 miles (3km) south to Seagrove Beach. Turn right onto **SR 30A** and head east.*

Seaside

8 This summer village of pastel-colored, traditionally styled wooden houses, straight out of Cape Cod, was actually created in 1985. The Victorian-style fretwork and white picket fences set off the pretty colors perfectly. Though contrived, this is a pleasant place to visit; just don't expect too much atmosphere and you won't be disappointed. Ironically, adjacent to Seaside is Grayton Beach, one of the oldest townships on Florida's Gulf Coast. There is a picturesque state recreation area here offering hiking, swimming, surf fishing and boating.

*Follow **SR 30A** northwest to the village of Santa Rosa Beach and continue west on **US 98** for 16 miles (26km) for Destin.*

Destin

9 Before you reach Destin (8 miles/13km), the road divides: the Beach Highway leads to the **Museum of the Sea and Indian**.

Destin has been renowned for its fishing since its foundation in the 1830s and is one of Florida's major sport fishing resorts. The most abundant trophy is billfish (which includes such varieties as spearfish, sailfish and marlin). It is perhaps no surprise, therefore, to find out that there is a **Fishing Museum** in town and that the restaurants here are highly regarded for their seafood. The most pleasant stretch of sand is **Crystal Beach Wayside Park**, 5 miles (8km) east of Destin. Visit the **Old Post Office Museum** for a look at local history.

ⓘ Destin Chamber of Commerce, US 98 East

Continue west for 7 miles (11km).

Okaloosa Island Beaches

10 At the eastern tip of Santa Rosa Island lies the beach playground for Fort Walton. The main attraction is **Gulfarium**. Dolphins and sea lions delight the crowds with their performances and there is a fine aquarium with many exotic deep-sea species.

*Cross the Intracoastal Waterway on **US 98** to the center of Fort Walton Beach and return to Pensacola via Gulf Breeze, 43 miles (69km).*

Pensacola–Museum of Naval Aviation **7 (11)**
Museum of Naval Aviation–Gulf Breeze Zoo **22 (35)**
Gulf Breeze Zoo–Santa Rosa Island **12 (19)**
Santa Rosa Island–Fort Walton Beach **16 (26)**
Fort Walton Beach–Eden Gardens **48 (77)**
Eden Gardens–Seaside **4 (6)**
Seaside–Destin **24 (39)**
Destin–Okaloosa Island Beaches **7 (11)**
Okaloosa Island Beaches–Pensacola **43 (69)**

SPECIAL TO . . .

Pensacola Each spring (late February/early March) Pensacola stages a fortnight of **Mardi Gras** festivities. Spectacular costume-and-mask parades take to the streets to the sound of jazz and samba and culminate in a grand Mardi Gras Ball. In May the city celebrates the **Fiesta of Five Flags**, which marks the settlement of the city in 1559 by Tristan de Luna. Locals don period costume and hold street fairs, and an old galleon sails into the port.

SCENIC ROUTES

On a sunny day the white sands and emerald waters edged by **SR 399** between Navarre Beach and Pensacola Beach make beautiful roadside scenery. To the north of Choctawhatchee Bay, **SR 20** will show you the old north Florida of pinewoods and fishing shacks, free of tourism developments and heavy traffic. As you turn south on **SR 331** and cross the bay, you will enjoy the sight of river barges and yachts cruising to and from the Intracoastal Waterway.

RECOMMENDED WALKS

The walking tour outlined on the previous pages for the historic Pensacola districts covers only the main points of interest. If you would like a comprehensive self-guided walking tour of this fascinating area, ask for the brochure at the Pensacola Chamber of Commerce. For beachside strolls and hikes try the pine flatwoods and scrub of **Grayton Beach State Recreation Area** or **Gulf Islands National Seashore** (ask at the information center for details of trails).

INDEX

ACKNOWLEDGEMENTS

The Automobile Association would like to thank the following photographers, libraries and associations for their help in the preparation of this book.

J ALLAN CASH PHOTOLIBRARY   20 Hialeah PK Racecourse, 97 St Augustine, oldest house.

ALLSPORT/J GUND   84 Daytona Race track.

FLORIDA DEPARTMENT OF COMMERCE   103 Shrimp boats, 109 Sunset, 112 Panama City Beach, 115 Penascola Beach, 117 Deep sea fishing.

C HEARD   96 St Augustine, 101 Fire Department, St Augustine.

P MURPHY   75 Wildlife, 81 Winter Park, Morse Gallery, 87 Bowleys Café, Silver Springs, 95 St Augustine Spanish Quarter, 97 Oldest Store Museum, 98 Flagler College, 103 Fernandina Beach, 105 St George Street, 114 Wakulla Springs.

PICTURES COLOUR LIBRARY LTD   Cover Riviera Beach.

SPECTRUM COLOUR LIBRARY   19 Miami Beach, 24 Airboat, Everglades, 3 Duval Street.

WALT DISNEY CO   (Copyrighted) 2 Sorcery in the Sky, 5 Magic Kingdom, 67 Mickey Mouse, 71 Cinderella's Castle, Mickey Mouse, 72 Thunder Mountain, Railroad, 72 Spaceship Earth & Monorail, 73 Great Movie ride – Aliens, Indiana Jones – Stunt Theatre, 74 Typhoon Lagoon, Pleasure Island.

ZEFA PICTURE LIBRARY (UK) LTD   11 CenTrust Tower, Vizcaya House.